WHAT PEOPLE ARE SAYING ABOUT *SMALL BALL BIG RESULTS*

"Joel Goldberg is a natural storyteller, and there is an inspirational message behind every chapter in this home run of a book. This is not as much a story of Joel's storied career as a Major League Baseball broadcaster as it is about the leadership lessons we can learn from the small things that occur in our lives. Be ready to walk up to the plate and get inspired by his Small Ball stories that provide big-league wisdom."

John Gronski
Major General, U.S. Army (Retired)

"It's been a privilege to be able to work with Joel as long as I have in my career. Every player in that locker room enjoyed and respected Joel as a reporter. I'm walking away from the Royals with a lot of great memories with him, but an even better friendship!

To be a successful athlete and team, it's all about doing the small things that go unnoticed but add up to big results. This kind of approach is what led the Royals to a World Series championship. It took everyone in the organization, from players like myself to people in the media like Joel.

Joel has always been a great broadcaster and storyteller, and I know this book will continue to prove that!"

Alex Gordon
Eight-Time Gold Glove Winner, Kansas City Royals 2007-2020

i

"It might be easy—understandable even—to assume that a book entitled Small Ball is all about baseball strategy. The old adage about not judging a book by its cover comes to mind, however. *Small Ball Big Results* introduces us to fascinating people whose lives, in one way or another, personify the lessons of baseball. We may strike out more than we homer, but as long as we keep swinging, we have a chance to be champions. Joel Goldberg's effort is as exciting as a well-executed squeeze play that scores the winning run in the bottom of the ninth in game seven of the World Series. Break out the champagne!"

Sly James
Former Mayor, Kansas City, Missouri

"Small Ball is taking baby steps and building big-picture pieces. It's paying attention to detail and knowing what you want to accomplish before you set out to do it. I've traveled with Joel Goldberg and he always has interesting stories. I'm glad they can now be read in *Small Ball Big Results*."

George Brett
MLB Hall of Fame

"With a gift for storytelling that puts a smile in your face and makes you want to lean in to listen more closely, Joel Goldberg tackles the big topic of Small Ball. As leaders we make important and consequential decisions all the time, but our legacy and our true impact are tied to the little things we intentionally do day in and day out, the Small Ball. I know that you will be inspired and encouraged when you lean in and hear these Small Ball stories. Once you read one, you'll be eager to hear Joel tell you the next one!"

Susana Eshleman
President and CEO, Children International

"Negro Leagues founder Andrew "Rube" Foster demanded a style of play that deployed tactics like the bunt and run with timely hitting and aggressive base running. Some would call it Small Ball. I call it winning baseball. Author Joel Goldberg has masterfully taken those same principles that Rube preached and applied them to a must-read book to help businesses win by doing the little things that get big results."

Bob Kendrick
President, Negro Leagues Baseball Museum

"Small Ball Big Results contains some very valuable jewels that took many of us far too long to learn. If you are reading and listening carefully, you will gain a great deal from Joel's book."

Barnett Helzberg, Jr.
Chairman and Founder of the Helzberg Entrepreneurial Mentoring Program

"In *Small Ball, Big Results*, Joel Goldberg reminds us that simply taking care of the little things can make a big impact on the lives of those in our community, in our families, and on our teams. A winning culture goes far beyond wins and losses."

Dayton Moore
Sr. Vice President/General Manager, Kansas City Royals

"A belief in the importance of the word "team" is critical when it comes to success in sports, business and life. Joel Goldberg's Small Ball Big Results highlights lessons learned through team successes and team losses. His collection of superstars and role models showcase why being surrounded by a team is so important. We can all hit home runs if we focus on people, positivity and doing the right thing. His stories from the locker room to the board room provide practical and important advice. I'm proud to call him a friend and mentor as I read his stories."

Kathy Nelson
President/CEO, Kansas City Sports Commission & Foundation

"Joel has hit it out of the park with *Small Ball Big Results*. Read it once for pleasure. Keep it within arm's reach and read it again and again. It will transcend your knowledge and transform your thinking. It is a way of doing and being that will elevate your career."

Mark LeBlanc, CSP
Author of *Never Be the Same* and *Growing Your Business!*

"*Small Ball Big Results* creatively captures life's journey. The top of the inning (the journey) may come with a set of challenges, while the bottom of the inning causes us to pivot. This book shows us that no matter the inning, we still need to finish the game! The stories in Small Ball Big Results show us that—no matter what happens—enjoy the journey."

Dr. Kimberly Beatty
Chancellor, Metropolitan Community College, Kansas City

"Aspects of cohesive relationships, trust and love of each other… these can only be expressed over time within a culture of sports or business. Joel Goldberg brings this to the light in *Small Ball Big Results*. Great sport coaches learn these small things take time but produce big results. Oh my, in a capitalist society how we need to bring the heart into the business sector. Small Ball Big Results does just that!"

Dr. Jeff Duke
Founder, 3D Institute

SMALL BALL **BIG** RESULTS

JOEL GOLDBERG

ISBN-13: 978-1-7362389-0-5

Editor: Paige DeRuyscher

Graphic Designer: Joni McPherson

TABLE OF CONTENTS

FOREWORD

I played baseball growing up. From as young as I can remember… hitting off a tee, to underhand pitches from the coach, to Little League, Babe Ruth, and high school. If I'm being honest, sport took priority over school work. As a result, I spent one post graduate year at Fork Union Military Academy after high school graduation to play baseball and "get my stuff together." For most of my baseball playing days I was a catcher—great bat, average arm and slow as a turtle! But it was from this vantage point that I gained appreciation for how all of the very small details of the game could be beautifully choreographed into a winning team. Knowing the exact right time to visit the pitching mound, positioning the outfield just a few more steps to the right, that certain glance at the runner on first just so he knew I was paying attention, picking up clues from the third-base coach from my peripheral vision, connecting to our shortstop without words to make that unexpected throw to second base.

When I first met Joel Goldberg, I knew he was not your "typical sports broadcaster." We had been paired up for an event at a local technology organization and he was to interview me about my arrival to Kansas City and H&R Block. I found his questions to be rich and insightful. He had a way of probing to help the audience learn more about me while at the same time putting me at ease. He moved deftly between sport and business, oftentimes drawing parallels that helped people connect and learn in interesting ways. Since that day, I've seen Joel leverage this gift to the advantage of all that listen.

Small Ball Big Results is like Joel Goldberg extra innings! Using metaphors from baseball and learnings from sport and business, Joel covers the topics most relevant to leaders today—being guided by purpose, building trust, the importance of talent, dealing with the uncertain and unexpected, and what it means to do the right thing, just to name a few. If you know Joel from the Kansas City Royals broadcasts, you'll relish in his savvy outside the lines. If you don't, *Small Ball Big Results* will be a fresh take on important topics that you'll want to give all members on your team.

Business, like baseball, is full of little decisions. And while strategy clearly has its role, the move from being good to great comes to those who can orchestrate and execute in the most finessed and precise way. That's what *Small Ball Big Results* is all about. Retail is detail, after all.

Jeffrey J. Jones II
President & CEO
H&R Block

PREGAME

As a kid, I dreamed of working at Major League Baseball stadiums, specifically of being a first baseman for the Philadelphia Phillies. I remember hitting dramatic game seven World Series wiffle ball home runs in the backyard of my parents' house in Moorestown, New Jersey. I quickly realized early on that my career path would not involve me doing anything in terms of playing sports. I was a mediocre athlete, to put it mildly, but I sure loved to talk about sports. I drove my teachers, parents and anyone who spent time around me crazy with my constant need to recap the previous night's baseball, football, hockey or basketball games. I used to turn down the volume on the television and call games at home, hoping one day I might be the announcer. I never thought that I would become friends with the likes of George Brett, Willie Wilson, John Wathan or Dennis Leonard and get to work with broadcast partners like Frank White, Jamie Quirk and Paul Splittorff. All of them played in the first memorable and impactful World Series of my childhood, albeit for the Kansas City Royals who would take on *my* Phillies. I learned more about the game from Frank, Splitt and Jamie than anyone in my lifetime...and not just about strategy. They taught me about teamwork, people, and all the elements needed to win on the field and in the game of life.

As Negro League Baseball's legend Buck O'Neil once said, "Nothing better than baseball. It teaches all the lessons."

I didn't understand this as a young broadcaster, climbing the ladder in small markets working as a sports reporter on the news. I'm not sure I even grasped it while covering the Cardinals in the World Series during my tenure in St. Louis. Baseball is so similar to life because it takes place day after day, five to seven times per week. Good or bad, win or lose, the game, like life, continues. I came to grasp that when I moved my family to Kansas City in 2008 and worked every local televised game, traveling with the team all across the country. I started to learn about organizational culture, teamwork, resilience and doing things the right way as I grabbed a front row seat to observe as the struggling Royals built a championship.

I spent my offseasons broadcasting some college and prep games, but never really felt fulfilled in the winter. In December 2016, I announced a high school basketball tournament in Columbia, Missouri, and went to dinner afterward with my friend and Secretary of State at the time, Jason Kander, his wife Diana and their son, True.

Jason and I had become friends over a mutual love of baseball and we chatted often. His life changed as he became a prominent figure in the world of politics, making an impact locally and nationally...but he also affected my life that night. Jason and Diana asked me about my offseason, and I told them about some games I had scheduled to broadcast and an upcoming speech to a lawn care and golf course management association. They wondered if I spoke to groups often and I replied, "no." Jason then suggested, "You know, you could build a speaking business." I will admit that the idea seemed preposterous. I thought professional speakers were Tony Robbins. Plus, I had never spent a day in the corporate world. But I had, with inside access to leadership every day of my career, observed some of the best strategists and competitors in sports. I credit the Kanders for planting the seed. Diana, a speaker herself, pointed me in all the right directions. I hired a speaking coach and a writing consultant for my speeches. But I needed to meet people in the business world.

My good friend and neighbor, Casey Wright, owner of a recruiting firm, told me I needed to network. I asked, "What's networking?" Hey, I had been networking my whole life, but we don't call walking around the locker room "networking." Casey introduced me to Scott Havens, one of the top connectors in Kansas City. *He* introduced me to executives and set up free speeches with crowds of 50 guests at a time, essentially allowing me to showcase my abilities and meet influential decision makers.

I also started a podcast called *Rounding The Bases* with a goal of interviewing leaders and entrepreneurs. The hope was to expand my brand beyond baseball, grow my network and develop content from the business world. I rarely spoke about sports during the interviews, preferring to focus on business and leadership. But sports seemed to intrigue audiences. I asked Pat Williams why during one of my podcasts. He was one of my rare sports guests, having spent half a century working in the National Basketball Association. Williams had drafted future NBA legends like Charles Barkley and Shaquille O'Neal and agreed to sit down with me one morning in Orlando. I made the drive from St. Petersburg, Florida just hours before working a Royals-Tampa Bay Rays game. His observation: "We live in a sports-crazy nation. This country of ours is absolutely addicted to sports at all levels and the athlete, the coach, the broadcaster—those who are in the profession, definitely have a huge sphere of influence."

So I started asking each of my guests three baseball-themed questions: *What is the biggest home run you've hit professionally? What is the biggest swing and miss you've taken and what did you learn from it?*

And, the one that inspired this book: *What is Small Ball, or the small bunts and hits that lead to wins?*

In baseball and business, everyone wants to hit the home run, but I've watched successful teams like the 2015 World Champion Kansas City Royals win with speed, defense, relief pitching and character. The home runs came, but they won by playing Small Ball. In listening to the stories from the thousands of interviews I've done in locker rooms and boardrooms, I've come to understand that champions master the little things.

Dr. Michelle Robin, a wellness champion, chiropractor, author, friend and podcast guest of mine, wrote in her book *Small Changes Big Shifts*, "Trust in your journey and take the next step, and then the next."

This made me think of my longtime television broadcast partner Jeff Montgomery. Drafted by the Cincinnati Reds in the ninth round in 1983, the odds were stacked against "Monty" when he started his minor league baseball career. Surrounded by highly regarded prospects who stood out more than he did in terms of talent and stature (5'11", 170 for a right-handed pitcher doesn't generally open eyes on the baseball diamond), a 21-year-old Montgomery received words of encouragement from a coach who told him if he just worked hard at getting a little better every day, he might make it. Jeff Montgomery spent offseasons working on mechanics in the mirror at home and finished his career as the Royals all-time saves leader. He's one of 30 pitchers in baseball history with 300 or more saves. Monty succeeded in baseball and in life by playing Small Ball.

Granted a level of access to CEOs and business leaders while simultaneously speaking with the highest level of athletes and coaches has put me in a position to share Small Ball perspectives.

As Williams told me, "We should always be on the lookout for good quotes. Good anecdotes, good quips, good stories. The world is not made up of atoms, Joel. It's made up of stories."

I hope you enjoy the tales told in the pages ahead. Each chapter—or "inning"—features a business and baseball story pertaining to various Small Ball topics meant to inspire you to focus on the little things that add up to the home runs in life.

1 PURPOSE

TOP OF THE 1ST

Getting ready to board a plane to go on vacation following the 2008 baseball season, a man approached me at Kansas City International Airport. He asked if I was the baseball announcer on TV. Having just completed my first season with the Royals, it felt good to be recognized as the new guy in town. He told me he liked my work, but then made a comment that caught me off-guard: "You do a great job, but I feel sorry for you." Perplexed, I asked why, and he suggested it must be rough "talking about all those losses every night."

Sure, the Royals had finished with 75 wins and 87 losses, but I quickly answered, "Don't feel sorry for me! I'm living my dream. Can you believe they pay me to talk about baseball?" I was sincere, but at that point, the thought about "purpose" had never entered my mind. Thirteen years into my television career, getting airtime every night and playing a significant role had me on cloud nine. Although, truth be told, I was playing the "finite game"—something author Simon Sinek refers to in his book, *The Infinite Game*. The *infinite* game involves big picture thinking, purpose, advancing a just cause and building trusting teams. The *finite* game focuses on wins and losses...and early in my inaugural season with the Royals, I felt more

1

like a fan, getting excited about the victories and frustrated with the defeats. I liked the players and wanted to see them succeed, so the losses bummed me out.

Then one night my new broadcast teammate Paul Splittorff gave me some advice. Splitt (we never called him Paul) might be the best broadcaster I ever worked with. As a pitcher, the hard-nosed lefty played his full 15-year career for KC and holds the franchise record for wins. What made him so special after he left the field (along with a strong work ethic and deep knowledge of the game) is that he served as a television analyst for part of each game and the play-by-play announcer for the rest. Almost all former players serve as color commentators, but Splitt could handle either role perfectly. He would later move out of the booth in 2009 when a health issue affected his speech. Determined to keep such a beloved local figure on the broadcasts, Fox Sports and the Royals shifted Splitt to be my pregame and postgame show analyst. Legendary Royals second baseman Frank White, who I'd built spectacular chemistry with, was then shifted to the booth. The thinking was that Splitt would only have to talk for parts of a half-hour show instead of a full game. I never would've wanted that to be the reason I was sitting beside Splitt, but selfishly, I relished calling this tough-yet-gentle, serious-but-witty father figure my partner before he passed due to cancer in May of 2011.

But back in 2008, a healthy Splitt pulled me aside after another bad loss and said, "There are a lot of important people that are paid to lose sleep over these losses. You're not one of them." On the surface, that might sound like he told me not to care, which couldn't have been further from the truth. Rather, the message was *win or lose, you have a role to play and a job to do.* Don't let the down times affect your ability to talk about baseball. It took me a while, and I watched in amazement as Splitt and his partner, Ryan Lefebvre, could so effortlessly take the emotion out of the result while still providing the energy and passion for the game of baseball. Splitt's words helped me grow and begin to understand the purpose we all served.

As social media grew over the years, I would regularly receive messages from fans who would describe a loved one struggling with their health. Something along the lines of, "My mom is in hospice and all she wants to do is watch you guys on TV." Stories about memories of baseball with "my late father," or tweets from service members overseas commenting on the amazing game the night before. Oftentimes, the game being referenced was far from amazing. *A blowout loss and a three-hour rain delay? Not so amazing,* I would think. But I learned that the results mattered much less to those abroad. Soldiers would wake up in the middle of the night just to see a piece of home. I came to appreciate that a win or a loss paled in comparison to my purpose of bringing people all over the world some joy, a diversion or a little connectivity.

In 2018, the team and the network asked me if I would fly to the Middle East on a USO Tour to visit the troops. I had missed only one televised game in 11 seasons due to my grandfather passing away, but I couldn't turn down the assignment of a lifetime. Former Royals players Mike Sweeney, Reggie Sanders, Bret Saberhagen and Hall of Fame third baseman George Brett made the trip...and I would chronicle every moment, including watching a September 11 Royals game being played back in Kansas City alongside some of the men and women stationed at Camp Buehring in Kuwait. We had done numerous Armed Forces Night broadcasts over the years on 9/11 from Kauffman Stadium while interviewing soldiers via satellite during a game, but now I would be the one *on* satellite with the troops. Arriving on the evening of September 10 and waking up in a Kuwait City hotel the next morning, hours before Americans would rise on such a somber day back in the states, hit me with a powerful emotion I can't fully describe.

It occurred to me that George Brett could go anywhere around the world and stay in the most luxurious resort with his baseball status. So, why venture into the 120-degree heat of the desert? "These guys leave for six months, eight months, years at a time and some of them have been doing it for 20, 30 years. If they can go out, the least I can do is take five days out of my schedule," Brett said. Plus, the military has always been close to his heart. "My father was a tank driver in World War II and got wounded pretty bad, so I'm lucky I'm even here," Brett told me. Ironically, he met a man from Emporia, Kansas during our trip who ran the tank division. George promised to visit him when the young man returned to the states.

Soldiers oooh-ed and ahh-ed over Brett's credentials all trip long, but I heard him tell them all the same message over and over during our stay: "Everybody makes a big deal about getting 3,000 hits. I made 7,000 outs. I don't know how many errors I made, don't know how many times I struck out with the bases loaded in the eighth inning. But I will tell you if you make an error in the military...if you make 7,000 outs in the military...if you strike out with the bases loaded in the eighth or ninth inning, chances are you're coming home in a wooden box." Baseball is one thing, but Brett wanted those men and women to know their sacrifice meant *everything*.

We ate with the troops, took tours, climbed into helicopters and fired weapons simulators. Before we could thank the men and women for their service, they would all thank us for the visit. We received a hero's welcome from true heroes. Forget about the jet lag. This was special. "I feel like family," Sanders, the longtime MLB outfielder, said proudly.

Saberhagen spoke to a group of soldiers who weren't much older than he was when he made his big-league debut in 1984 as a 19-year-old pitcher and won the World Series MVP award as a 21-year-old. "As much as you guys are enjoying this, I think we are enjoying this even more."

Capt. Aaron Shaffer told me sometime around 2:30 a.m., "It's awe inspiring, really, to see what these players are doing. They signed up for this. They volunteered for this just like we volunteered for our jobs." Moments later, 200 of us stood in a room singing the Star-Spangled Banner at 3 a.m. local time before first pitch, then enjoyed America's pastime while sitting 16 miles from the Iraqi border and some 7,000 miles from home. A standing ovation broke out as the

Royals won the game on the big screen television at 6:13 in the morning. I walked outside to do a postgame interview, not with the player of the game (my usual role), but with Sgt. Nick Ledet, a kid I had meshed with instantly. Saberhagen and Sweeney dumped a bucket of Gatorade over Ledet as the sun came up, and Ledet's family watched back home that night in Kansas. Months later, my wife and I would take Nick's wife and baby daughter to dinner in Kansas City, Facetiming Sgt. Ledet in the desert during our meal. Now that he's back home safely, Nick and I catch up in person from time to time and message one another frequently.

I asked him at one point why he served. What was his purpose? He says he thought often about this while on patrol in Syria. "My dad served for 27 years. I wanted to follow the family tradition," he shared. "I feel like I'm a patriot. I love this country. We have our divides, but what makes it great is we get to be free. I get to fight and serve for that freedom. I had the privilege to be able to sign up."

I felt chills as Nick told me that...the same feeling I experienced as I departed Kuwait with a full heart, an emotion Mike Sweeney described when the trip ended: "Looking into a soldier's eyes and giving them a hug from their wife and kids back home...I've never been more proud to be an American," Sweeney said. "This trip has forever shaped my life."

I think about that trip often. And about another hero I met overseas named Maj. Travis Neely, a die-hard Royals fan who told me in an emotional live interview during the game that the families back home were the true heroes. "We're simply soldiers who show up and do what we're told to do."

Reminds me of Splitt. Do your job, win or lose. When he passed on May 25, 2011, I was called on to host a special tribute show a couple days later from Arlington, Texas, before the Royals played the Texas Rangers. Somehow fighting off tears, we shared the memories of our friend and colleague Paul Splittorff with our audience. I stayed strong and did my job the way Splitt would have expected. Years later, I understand that I achieved my purpose on that painful but important day.

BOTTOM OF THE 1ST

We often hear the phrase "Family is everything," but when you meet a family like the Hansons, you understand that expression in a whole new way. You can't help but be warmed by their kindness, uplifted by their humor, and inspired by the story of what three people can do together for the world.

Jeff Hanson was born September 30, 1993 in Overland Park, Kansas with a genetic condition called neurofibromatosis, which causes tumors to form on nerve tissue. By age six, Jeff's parents, Julie and Hal, learned that he had a brain tumor; by 12, it had severely damaged his vision. Hal recalls, "As a parent, you decide to have a child and you have a bank of dreams of what your child is going to become someday." He speaks of all those typical things a father might hope for a son—to be a quarterback, an astronaut, President of the United States. And when the news is delivered that he will grow up with physical limitations, some of those dreams are taken away. As more medical problems emerge, more dreams are gone until, "Finally," he says, "you get to the point where your dream bank is almost empty."

Hal recalls the lowest point he can remember, sitting one night with his son on the patio, looking through an old telescope. "I was trying to show him the moon and Mars and some simple things. He looked up at the sky with his eyes and asked, 'Can you just see stars when you look up?'" He realized that Jeff couldn't see one of them. Hal continues, "I sat outside and cried and thought, '*Where is this headed?*'"

He asked the question in Jeff's 12th year of life, just as weeks of chemo and radiation started. But something remarkable happened that same year—the discovery of Jeff's artistic talent. During treatments, Jeff began to paint to pass the time. "And that," says his dad proudly, "is where the story really began."

Today, Jeff is a world-renowned artist, the head of the Hanson family business, and a philanthropist who has raised millions for charity. And he knows he hasn't done it alone. "We're a great team," Jeff says of the dynamic trio made up of his mom, dad and him. The journey they've taken together is one you won't soon forget.

Here's how it all happened. The summer following Jeff's treatment, the family remodeled his bedroom and Jeff decided it was missing one item: the perfect chair. While shopping, he set his sights on a particular leather chair—which happened to be $1,300. Not wanting to deter his dream, Jeff's parents encouraged him to save up for it... and that's when the idea of Jeff's Bistro was born. The determined 12-year-old decided he would spend the summer selling lemonade and baked goods at the foot of the driveway to earn enough for that chair. On the day of his fourth Bistro, a generous neighbor who'd admired his effort had the chair of Jeff's dreams delivered to his house. The neighbor encouraged Jeff to use this as an opportunity to pay it forward—to continue raising funds, but for others. His mom, Julie, says that was one of the most pivotal points on Jeff's journey, and a huge lesson for the family about generosity and purpose.

So, Jeff's Bistro grew into a thriving fundraiser for neurofibromatosis research. Soon, along with daily treats, he was selling the watercolor notecards he'd painted during chemotherapy. As people pulled up for their coffee and pastries on the way to work, Jeff would be sitting there at the foot of the driveway painting more. Hal remembers vividly seeing his son at that little table, working so intently, his face just a few inches from the picture due to his extremely low vision.

"We learned that Jeff's heart was enormous," Julie says. "His heart for others and his kindness ...was even bigger than the art." The little jar Jeff put out to collect donations for the Children's Tumor Foundation filled up constantly as money poured in, and they soon witnessed the truth that "generosity begets generosity." "We quickly learned that it's more blessed to give than to receive," Julie smiles. By the end of the summer, Jeff had generated $15,000 for the foundation.

Not only that, but Jeff's art was drawing notice and not just because it was done by a visually impaired boy. People admired it and started to request his work. When his eye doctor suggested that he try working with a larger canvas, he gave it a shot. Jeff's first canvas painting sold for $400 at a charity auction.

Just three years later, Hal questioned his 15-year-old son, "How much money are you making selling these paintings?" Jeff's answer blew him away: $35,000. Hal laughs, "I said, 'Holy cow you're gonna have to file income tax!'" He adds, "At this point, I still couldn't believe that they were buying his art because they liked the art." It wasn't until Jeff turned 20 that Hal truly realized people weren't just feeling sorry for his son; they loved his work, even without knowing his story.

But as successful as they've been, the road hasn't always been smooth. The Hansons have had to learn how to get through tough times, together, and this family truly knows that laughter is the best medicine. And thankfully, it's the way Jeff is wired: "Laughter was *everything* during treatment," Julie says. "There's never been a time when I so craved humor and laughter."

"Jeff was bound and determined to not be defined by, '*That's the blind kid down the street with the brain tumor*,'" Hal adds. Hal suggests a good dose of silliness for anyone going through adversity—doing crazy, zany things, watching funny videos—whatever it takes to forget your own struggles for a while and get through with a smile.

Here's a perfect example: After 28 days of radiation therapy, Jeff showed up for his last session in a get-up that made everyone's day.

At that point, most people just look forward to ringing a bell and being done with it all, but not this guy. He was dressed to the nines in a top hat and tuxedo. Jeff loved the thought that no one had ever done something like that before, and, of course, his parents supported him wholeheartedly. (What's $100 to rent a tux when you're making a life-long memory?) But they went above and beyond: "I filled the yard with the brightest signs that said, 'Continue Praying For Jeff,' 'Kindness Wins,' and 'Thank You, Friends,'" Julie smiles at the memory. When Jeff returned from treatment, the yard was packed with family and friends holding helium balloons for a balloon launch. Ten minutes later, a limousine pulled up to complement the tuxedo and to help make that day one Jeff would never forget.

Hal calls it "a pivotal moment in his treatment and the journey we were on." It was an illustration of who his son has always been: "His definition wasn't about the disease; it was about his personality…He was bound and determined not to be defined by his challenge, but by his *response* to the challenge."

Today, Jeff has a successful art business at 27. And by "successful," I mean his paintings hang on the walls of the likes of Bill Gates, George Lucas, Billie Jean King, Glenn Close, John Cena, Susan Sarandon, Billy Joel and Jack Black…to name a few. Even more importantly to the Hansons, at just 18 years old, Jeff reached his goal to raise $1 million for charity, raised $5 million by age 25, and Jeff says confidently, "My current goal is to raise $10 million by the time I'm 30."

"This wasn't about having some elaborate business plan," Hal says. "This organically grew from encouraging a kid to focus on what you *can* do, not what you can't do. Focus on your *ability* not your disability."

The Hansons are a small but mighty team, working together to share Jeff's beautiful, original paintings with the world. How do they do

it, living and working under one roof? "We have well-defined roles," Julie says.

"Jeff is our boss," Hal adds, regarding his son's role as Creative Director of the business. "He is the painter; I'm the painter's assistant and gopher; Julie is the manager and marketer." As you might imagine, this family has a knack for having fun together, dreaming big, and constantly looking for ways to grow the business and reach more people with their generosity.

One of the most delightful stories of Jeff's journey thus far involves his unique request for the Make-a-Wish Foundation—to meet Elton John. It was a rare request from someone of Jeff's generation, and the only Make-a-Wish Elton had ever granted. The foundation didn't exist in the '70s when the music star was a teenage heartthrob. Jeff smiles, "I walked in with $1,000 for his foundation. And not to be outdone, he reciprocated with a $5,000 check to Children's Tumor Foundation...and a first-class trip to Dubai to see a concert there."

Julie adds, "The minute Jeff gave Elton a hug, it was like he was his favorite nephew."

Hal laughs, "I was the most star-struck because I'm closer to Elton's age. I was staring at his shoes and his glasses and his costume and thinking, *Oh my gosh, this is Elton John!*"

What they thought would be two minutes and a few pictures turned into a heartfelt connection and the beginning of a special friendship. Julie remembers, "Within 10 minutes he was crying to us, sharing about his childhood." She saw how it touched him to spend time with "normal people"—a rock star who'd been famous for well over 50 years, always scheduled to meet some big name in the Green Room. Here was this little family from Kansas, and he wanted a piece of their world for just that snippet of time. "He craved hearing about our lives," Julie says. Seeing the closeness of their family and the way they'd poured into their son with special needs surely left a lasting impression on the singer.

The signature Hanson humor comes out when they recall Elton's next invitation, this one to his show in Las Vegas. Hal recalls Elton's words: "I'll fly you there, we can hang out and go to dinner again and you can see the show." He laughs incredulously, "Elton John turns to his attendant and says...'Let's look at my calendar and their calendar and we'll find a date.' So, Elton gives us a photocopy of his calendar, and it says things like, *'Play piano at Nelson Mandela's 90th birthday party.'* And ours said, like, *'Hal has a haircut at 12:30.'"* Needless to say, they were able to make it happen, and as Jeff recalls about the whole experience with the iconic singer, they made "memories of a lifetime."

Whether rubbing elbows with superstars, being featured on national television shows like *CBS Sunday Morning* or speaking on a local podcast (mine!), the Hansons always have grateful hearts, and they share that gratitude with those around them. "Our family strongly believes in the power of the handwritten note...it's a lost art," Julie says. "Jeff has been holding an ink pen in his hand from the first moment he could, and for him to write a note is a big deal—a much bigger deal than those of us with normal vision." She believes that taking the time for that personal connection makes a big impact, no matter who is doing the writing. She challenges others to give it a try: "I encourage people to think about writing one note a week."

I have two of my own handwritten Jeff Hanson thank you notes and both are treasures, the messages equally as beautiful as the hand-painted designs on the cards. Those notes made my day. *This* is Jeff Hanson's purpose. He brings joy and inspiration to everyone he comes into contact with, whether it be in person or through his art. I think we all need those little reminders to go the extra mile for one another.

People everywhere have been touched by the story of this young man from Kansas who's on a mission to change the world through art. Jeff's dad marvels at how far the family has come together: "I didn't have any more dreams at all for Jeff—and now, 13 years later, I quit my emergency room doctor job and I work for him. This is the kid who I thought wouldn't find meaningful work, or a purpose."

He calls it "an unbelievable turn of events that's Jeff-driven but...also God-driven."

Jeff's mom agrees and offers a bit of advice for others: "Look at what you do really well and what brings you joy every day. By doing that, you will live the most joyful life on this earth."

It's a beautiful illustration of a Small Ball secret: *Find a way to live out your purpose, and never settle for less.*

② PEOPLE

TOP OF THE 2ND

In January of 2020 I sat down with Lisa Ginter, CEO of Kansas City's CommunityAmerica Credit Union (CACU) to talk about Small Ball. It was just 20 days before the Kansas City Chiefs won the Super Bowl, a game Ginter would attend. More on that in a moment...

The *National Business Journal* named Ginter one of the top 100 financial executives in 2019. She has worked for CACU for more than 25 years and after taking over as CEO, Lisa grew the credit union from a $1.5 billion to a nearly $4 billion organization in just five years. Most importantly, I've come to learn she stands out because of her love for people.

At my first lunch meeting with Lisa, she spoke about creating and passing on value to the credit union's members, passionately expressing the importance of relationships in business. I took notes, jotting down nuggets of wisdom, but what stood out to me and left an indelible impression was a simple, yet genuine offer minutes after she first met me: "What can I do to help *you*?" She would make me this offer regarding numerous topics, over and over again, from that day forward.

The second eldest of 10 siblings, Lisa felt the love and built-in support of a large family and always helped her parents with her youngest brothers and sisters. Having been a nurturer from a young age, she believes that CEOs should bring their hearts to their jobs. "People will work harder for somebody that they know is working really hard for them," she said. When Ginter was being considered for the top position at CACU, she was interviewed by the board and peppered with questions, including why she wanted the role. Without flinching, she told them she didn't want it for the three initials of C. E. O. Rather, she sought the job because those three letters would allow her to make a significant impact on the members, her employees, and the community. She calls CACU a people-driven organization and says the part she loves most about her job is "the love that we have for people. We're founded on the principle of people funding people."

She went on to say that building a strong foundation with highly invested and capable individuals in place is key: "I think the little things are just making sure that you assemble yourself with the right people. Talent is so important; people that believe in what you're about and your mission and your cause…don't skimp on that. We've got the foundation laid because we have the right talent. Those are what will get us the little base hits that turn into doubles that turn into the big wins."

Speaking of wins, CACU maintains a massive brand presence in Kansas City, and the most recognizable face in town serves as a CACU spokesman. When Chiefs quarterback Patrick Mahomes isn't completing jaw-dropping passes on the gridiron, he can be seen pitching the credit union. After being selected in the National Football League draft in April of 2017, the young quarterback's agent approached CACU about a one-year sponsorship deal. At this point, no one knew he would emerge as a soon-to-be Super Bowl Most Valuable Player and the face of the league nationwide. All Ginter knew was that she needed to get to know this person. She told the agent "Before I do anything, I want to meet the kid. I want to know what he's like, his personality, what's important to him." Ginter could not proceed with business without learning whether Mahomes' core values matched the credit union's.

When Ginter met with the young man who is the same age as her own kids, she asked him to talk about himself. She recalls, "In his raspy, cute voice he starts talking about his family." Mahomes was speaking her language because family is everything to her, and she knew in that moment a special partnership could develop. CACU was one of the first companies to sign the quarterback to an initial deal, and subsequently one of the first to agree with him to a multiple-year deal.

Perhaps Mahomes and Ginter also connect because of a will to win. Many of her employees describe her with some version of this statement: "Anybody who knows Lisa knows she goes big. Go big or go home." Translation: She throws deep touchdowns like the star quarterback. "You've got to take a risk...the way I look at things is if I'm going to go in, I'm going to put my chips all in."

Mahomes and Ginter also share a love of...you guessed it...people! On Mahomes standing up regularly in front of the media, she says, "He references 'we', his team. This isn't about Patrick; this is about the team. It's about the Chiefs. It's about how they're on this mission. It's just like an organization. We have this BEHAG (Big Empathetic Hairy Audacious Goal) and we're charging toward this visionary goal, and they have that, too. But you need somebody to make them believe in what they can do and that we can do this together."

Ginter prefers to describe Mahomes as the person over the player. "He is such a great kid, and I think just so grounded and humble." She experiences nerves at every Chiefs game like a family member would, and is like a second mom to him. As a matter of fact, Mahomes refers to Lisa as "Mama G." So many others in the Community America family feel the same way about her as a boss and loving influence.

Merriam-Webster defines the first word of the company Ginter runs as such:

Community: *A body of persons of common and especially professional interests scattered through a larger society.*

Her approximately 750 employees, the Chiefs, Mahomes and that community all matter. So does a large commitment to philanthropy and a committing heart to causes.

"If you keep people at the forefront of what you're doing and everything you do comes back to people, you're going to win this. You're going to win this game."

BOTTOM OF THE 2ND

Dayton Moore broke a rule he had set for himself when he drove to Dekalb-Peachtree Airport north of Atlanta in May of 2006 to meet with Kansas City Royals owner David Glass. Moore had vowed he would never interview for a job he had no intention of taking. After all, he knew he was a part of the Atlanta Braves' succession plan and could very well be the next general manager of one of baseball's most successful franchises. Yet, here he was. The Royals were his favorite boyhood team because of the annual summer visits to see his grandmother in Coldwater, Kansas, about 300 miles southwest of

Kansas City. Plus, he wanted to meet Mr. Glass (as nearly everyone called him), one of the most successful businessmen in the history of the United States.

Prior to buying the Royals in 2000, Glass served as the chief executive officer of Walmart from 1988 to 2000. During his 12-year tenure at the world's largest retailer, Glass increased annual revenue from $16 billion to $165 billion and was responsible for incorporating grocery inside its stores. In 1993 he was named most admired chief executive in the country in a *Fortune Magazine* peer survey.

Moore remembers an instant bond back at that airport meeting. "I connected with his heart and I found myself wanting this guy to do well." Glass opened up to Moore, upset about his baseball team's failures. They had compiled a record of 324 wins and 486 losses the previous five seasons, averaging 97 losses a year. Moore's Braves, during the same stretch, went 476-332, an average of 95 wins a season.

"One of the most successful businessmen in the history of our country was telling me that he had never failed this badly at something and he was embarrassed." Moore followed his heart and took the job.

Glass had built a reputation at Walmart as a servant leader. Quiet, private and respectful with an ever-present dash of humor, he always took an interest in others over himself. There to offer guidance, but never one to bark orders, he empowered his leaders. Good thing, because when Ned Yost took over as manager of the Royals in 2010, the often gruff and tough Yost wanted the freedom to do things his way. He said his previous job leading the Milwaukee Brewers involved a new owner discussing strategies until three in the morning. "When I got to Kansas City, I wasn't going to put up with an owner who was going to question everything that we did, complain about everything we did," Yost said. The two built a special bond and a shared demand for excellence. They could often be seen chit-chatting for long periods of time on the field during batting practice. "He knew that I was going to plain talk with him and he was going to plain talk with me...he'd walk into my office and he would say, 'Can I have a few minutes of your time?' And I would look at him and say, 'That depends on your attitude, doesn't it,' and he would laugh and sit down."

So imagine the scene on October 14, 2015. Final game of a playoff series between the Royals and Houston Astros. Winner advances, loser goes home. The fate of Kansas City rested in the arm of star pitcher Johnny Cueto, who Moore had acquired in a trade nearly three months before this season-deciding game. Cueto had been hot and cold with his performance and Glass sat in his Kauffman Stadium suite unable to calm his nerves—let alone the jitters of his family—about Cueto. "Hey, I'm going to go down and visit with Ned. Want to come?" he asked his son-in-law Phil Martz. The two ventured from the fifth floor to the first-floor locker room office of Yost and found the manager eating a sandwich. Remember, this was Yost, the man who didn't like meddling. Glass, not one to tell others how to do their job, simply asked about the choice of Cueto. Before the conversation could pick up steam, Yost stopped the owner in his tracks.

"Now, David, trust me. He's ready. He's got this," Martz remembers Yost saying in between sandwich bites. "That's what you came down for?" Yost asked incredulously. "You're wasting your time. We got this."

Martz called it the quickest meeting ever, and on the way back upstairs, turned to his father-in-law and said, "You really told him!" He then asked Glass why he even went down to Yost's office.

"I just wanted to get the family off my back," Glass replied. Cueto dominated that game, allowing just two runs over eight innings as the Royals beat the Astros with ease to advance on their way to an eventual World Championship.

I was not there for that conversation, but the story and answer about the family was Glass' classic dry humor. If I had a dollar for every time he faulted me for a Royals loss... "Well, Joel, I have to blame *someone*," he would say with a smile following the statement. The conversation always ended with, "You're doing a great job, Joel, keep it up."

When I started my speaking business in 2017, I was a little uneasy about doing something outside of my usual baseball job. I was free, contractually, to work on other projects, but I needed someone in my corner—some type of acknowledgment or approval that would give me the courage to branch out and try something new. At the Royals holiday party that year, Mr. Glass asked me what I'd been up to. When I told him what I wanted to pursue, his immediate response was, "That sounds like a great idea! Let me help you with it."

A weight was lifted for me that evening. I felt a sense of relief just knowing the guy who owned the team not only approved, but thought it was a smart idea. He saw my potential and helped me to see it, too. It was just the nudge I needed, and he knew it. That led to numerous conversations between us, and Mr. Glass started to do something that may seem small but made a big difference for me: he asked me how I was doing with my business every time he saw me. He made me feel like I was the most important person when I was in the room with him. But what I came to realize is that he made everyone feel that way.

Anyone in David Glass' world wanted to do right for him. The broadcasters, employees, players and even that gruff and tough manager who helped lead the franchise and city back to respectability in 2015. "The whole thrill and the joy was that we won the World Series for Mr. Glass, and to see him hold that trophy was probably the greatest moment in my career," Yost said to me years later, showing his sentimental side. "More than anything else because he stuck with us and he believed in us."

David, his wife, Ruth Ann, and the rest of the Glass family said goodbye on the final weekend of September 2019. They had just agreed to sell the team, and these would be their last games as owners. And once again, Mr. Glass slipped mostly under the radar, choosing to make Yost the focus. The franchise's winningest manager was set to retire at season's end. Glass, Moore and the organization wanted to honor the career of their leader, so Glass selflessly blended into the background. Mr. Glass did agree to sit down with my broadcast partner former All-Star reliever Jeff Montgomery and me to discuss his tenure with the Royals. He shared with us during the interview what I believe is the most important element of Small Ball.

"You do everything through people," he said. "If we all got paid on what we individually could produce, none of us would be worth very much. But if we can manifest our knowledge and our talents and so forth through other people, then [we] can win." He went on to say that this applies in all arenas—professional sports, the business world, whatever it is we endeavor to do, we have to do it through people.

In every interview I conducted with him through the years, I don't remember him ever saying "I did this" or "I did that." It was always about everyone else...never, ever about him. Just as Lisa Ginter had observed about Patrick Mahomes. David Glass didn't demand the spotlight, even though he certainly deserved it. He was the one who made sure to keep the sport of baseball in Kansas City when there was talk of possible contraction. He was the one who brought a title

back to KC. And when the time came to sell, he made sure to find an owner in John Sherman, who he knew cared about Kansas City. Outside investors from both coasts could've yielded an even larger price tag than the $1 billion sale.

Dayton Moore received a call on December 25, 2019, from Glass. "He sounded great, but I remember getting off the phone and thinking, '*I wonder if something is up.*'" The two always talked prior to Christmas but never on the actual holiday.

I called Mr. Glass in early January after the holidays to touch base and pick his brain. He always called back. Not this time. News broke that David Glass passed away from complications associated with pneumonia on January 9 at the age of 84.

Sweet, caring and ultra-competitive, David Glass often remarked with that hint of a smile, "Whoever said it doesn't matter whether you win or lose, it's how you play the game, was a loser." Or as he simply put it to me another time, "Losing is for losers."

He spoke with us about the disdain of losing in his final ever interview, "If you feel that way, *really* feel that way as much as I do, it makes winning all that much better."

David Glass was a winner. So were all the people whose lives he touched.

3 POSITIVITY

TOP OF THE 3RD

Rex Hudler played parts of 13 seasons in the major leagues and has spent the second part of his baseball career as a television analyst. Hud (no one calls him "Rex," including his wife, Jennifer) is the most energetic human I've ever met...let alone worked with. People ask me this one question about Hud all the time: "Is he really as crazy in person as on TV?"

My answer is always a definitive, "*Yes!*" And by "crazy," I mean wild and fun-loving in the very best ways.

Almost all of what we do as broadcasters covering Royals baseball is ad-lib. I don't like the term "winging it" because we spend time discussing and game-planning every day, but we don't follow a script. I know that for most of us, there's an element of "think first, speak second." We're reacting to developing storylines by the moment and mistakes are part of the deal with live television. But in general, we see, think and react. I'm pretty sure Hud falls more under the category of "speak first, think second." And I don't say that in a mean way at all. It absolutely works! It works because of his passion for the game and his love of people.

The result, though, is a daily dose of memorable phrases, which we've all come to enjoy thoroughly. Hud is like our modern-day Yogi Berra—the late Yankees Hall of Famer who was known for expressions like, "It ain't over till it's over," and "Baseball is 90 percent mental. The other half is physical." Those phrases were called "Yogiisms." Anytime Hud says something during a game that makes me or my partner Jeff Montgomery laugh hysterically or makes us stare at each other in disbelief, I jot down his exact words. We call them "Hudisms."

In a 2018 broadcast, Hud said, "Joel just used three big words in that report...'*Out of the box*'." And one beautiful afternoon in San Francisco at a Giants-Royals game, we showed a shot of a young fan eating ice cream. "Ice cream is not gonna melt on a 68-degree day," Hud stated. I mentioned to him later that his observation was not scientifically factual. Which is a perfect segue to the greatest Hudism hit of all-time when he called the moon "a beautiful planet." I could write an entire book of Hudisms. I point these out not to make fun of him, but to show how much fun he provides for all of us. Philosopher Hud he may not be, but of all the memorable life messages I've taken from Rex Hudler, none are more important than this:

There are energy-givers and energy-takers.

We find them in any locker room, office place...even in our homes. Have you ever considered which kind you are? Quite simply put, are you a person who turns on the light when you walk into a room, or do you pull down the shades? We, as human beings, naturally gravitate toward and feed off the positivity of an energy-giver.

For the better part of a decade, All-Star catcher Salvador Perez has been that constant energy giver in the Kansas City Royals clubhouse. He showed up in 2011 as a 21-year-old kid bouncing off the walls with contagious enthusiasm.

Sometimes his energy-giving shows itself in the form of celebratory Gatorade showers after wins. I don't know what happened to the day and age of high-fives and handshakes that we had growing up, but this generation's athletes seem to enjoy celebrating by dumping buckets of ice-cold water and Gatorade on each other after wins. In Kansas City, we call this the "Salvy Splash."

Photo Courtesy: John Sleezer, Kansas City Star

Photo Courtesy: John Sleezer, Kansas City Star

Photo Courtesy: John Sleezer, Kansas City Star

At some point several years ago, Salvy decided to dump a Gatorade bucket on a teammate while I was interviewing them after a game. Over time, this has evolved into a regular occurrence, and one that can be quite comical. I have been tasked so often with distracting

Photo Courtesy: John Sleezer, Kansas City Star

a player so Salvy could surprise them with a cold shower, I've joked that he deserves a director's credit for our broadcast because of the way he instructs me to position guests so they don't see him coming with the bucket!

These days, we have it down to an art. I've learned to just sneak a glance toward the dugout for a nonverbal signal from him so he can successfully execute his Salvy Splash. I guess I could say that I am an

Photo Courtesy: John Sleezer, Kansas City Star

accomplice...which means, in a small way, I get a chance to help him spread that positivity.

Through the highs and lows and the good times and bad, Salvy always seems to have a great day. In 2019 he missed the full season following elbow surgery. I really have not met a player who loves playing baseball as much as Salvy, so this news devastated him. Of course, his lows appear to be higher than most people's highs, but I could see it in his body language. He joined the team on the road in Boston later that season, not yet cleared to play but able to put on the catching equipment and start throwing. Just his presence, smile and infectious energy could be felt by all. He told me wearing his gear made him feel like Superman, and that it felt like his first day in the big leagues again. Day by day his health improved and that massive personality grew back to his one-of-a-kind self. Late in the season, I was standing on the field during batting practice in Chicago when I heard his voice close by. I looked over and saw Salvy standing in the first-base dugout recording an on-camera report, or "stand-up" as we say in the television business. No one had asked him to do this. My freelance photographer made sure to record when he saw Salvy grab the microphone. I watched his "report" afterward and suggested to our pre-game producer Casey Carter that we run the 20-second clip during the show. Salvy was suddenly a late addition to our rundown. "Royals Live from U.S. Cellular Field in Chicago. First game of the series. Joel doesn't want to work. Montgomery doesn't want to do anything today. So I'm going to help these guys because I'm not doing anything *all year long*! Okay, guys. We'll see you soon." Keep in mind, this is a man pretending to take over the role of on-camera reporter while speaking a second language with a mouthful of sunflower seeds. I'm not quite sure that every word mentioned was understandable, but this guy is beloved. What makes Salvy so special is that his energy-giving transcends any language barriers. While his grasp of the English language has grown every year, he's always had a way of spreading his energy through a radiant smile that is universally understood. That massive grin matches his large 6'3", 250-pound frame, making him the ultimate energy-giver. I'm pretty sure the only way Salvy could walk through town unnoticed is if Chiefs quarterback Patrick Mahomes were walking on the other side of the road taking the attention.

Now if Hudler and Perez are the two most energetic people I encounter on a daily basis at the ballpark, I know a woman who could undoubtedly play on the energy-givers' All-Star team.

I first met Sarah Nauser when she appeared on our pregame show August 8, 2018, prior to throwing out the first pitch before a Royals game. I have to be honest—knowing her story, I was worried about my emotions and possibly "losing it" on the air during the interview.

That never happened, because Sarah was never going to allow it. Not this incredibly upbeat young woman. The 29-year-old Kansas

City Police Department Officer had recently received a devastating diagnosis of ALS. She said the average lifespan after diagnosis is three to five years. When I asked her during the interview how she was doing she replied, "Day by day, new experience by new experience, it's been a blast." She kept mentioning the word "blast." Later on, one of Sarah's friends suggested that Montgomery and I looked smitten with Sarah on the air. How could we not be? She just smiled through the whole interview. She took pictures with us afterward, and then more while sitting on the dugout bench in between Royals manager Ned Yost and Hall-of-Famer George Brett. All three flashed big grins.

Fast forward to a week later when Montgomery, Carter, and I decided to spend a long rain delay at Kauffman Stadium visiting with Sarah and her friends. She was attending the game just one day after undergoing surgery to put a port in her chest. No complaints. Sarah just kept smiling. In fact, we found out that her nickname on the police force is "Smiley." She just has this way of uplifting everyone around her, an infectious ball of energy capable of brightening any situation. Well...anything outside of Mother Nature on a temperamental night. "I can't bring the sunshine all the time," Sarah laughed during the delay.

I've watched this young, beautiful, energetic woman make an impact on everyone she's come into contact with at the stadium. The red bracelet I'm wearing on the cover of this book reads, "Sarah's Soldiers" on one side and "Fight To Cure ALS" on the other. ABC featured Sarah nationally on the show *Nightline* in 2019, and she continues to inspire anyone lucky enough to come into contact with her. Former Royal Brett "Maverick" Phillips, another of her favorites, also clicked with Sarah. No surprise, because Maverick's energy level equals that of Salvy, Sarah and Hud. Sarah was upset when Phillips was traded from Kansas City to Tampa Bay on August 27, 2020. Phillips, perhaps the last man on the roster, was expected

to chip in if needed as a late game defensive replacement or pinch runner...until he suddenly found himself at the plate in game four of the World Series against the Los Angeles Dodgers. With two outs, two on and trailing by a run, an out would hand the Rays a loss and put them in a deep hole. Phillips delivered a hit, and an ensuing error on the play allowed not one run, but two to score as the Rays won in dramatic fashion. Sprinting around the field, his arms spread wide like the wings of an airplane, Phillips was a hero on the biggest of stages. He had been texting with Sarah back in Kansas City throughout the postseason.

Maverick describes her this way. "I look up to her and how she lives her life. Regardless of the circumstances in her life, she wakes up

every day finding something to feel blessed for and treats everyone around her with love and respect. I appreciate her and feel so thankful to know her!"

I've watched Sarah lose her ability to walk, so she scoots around in her wheelchair. I've watched her struggle at times to speak, so she texts, spreading the same joy as always. I've watched her fall in love with her boyfriend, Lonnie, equally as concerned about his well being as he is about hers. I have yet to see her positivity dwindle.

I texted her in November 2020, sending the picture she took with Monty and Me. I very rhetorically asked if she remembered it and inquired about how she was doing. "Of course, I do! It's on my wall!

I am doing great. I feel good and I'm optimistic that treatment will be here soon!"

She was planning an upcoming May wedding around the Royals schedule, wanting to make sure some of her baseball friends were at home.

"George is going to be the officiant LOL," she texted. By "George," she meant George Brett. The LOL was not meant to imply she was kidding. Just her smiling at the thought of the greatest player in the history of her favorite team officiating her wedding. She never could have dreamed of a life with ALS. She's not complaining, though. Sarah Nauser is an energy-giver, and George Brett will help her tie the knot. No, this was not what she expected.

Her reply, "Not in a million years, but how freaking cool."

BOTTOM OF THE 3RD

Wesley Hamilton is another positive force of nature. His smile alone will turn your day around, but his story will change the way you see what's possible in your life. Born on Kansas City's East Side in a neighborhood wrought with drugs, poverty and gun violence, Wesley had no plans to get out; his highest hope was to survive as long as possible, just like so many young men around him.

"I was raised by my mom…grew up with a mindset that the world had some type of chip on its shoulder for me. Not understanding that I had a chip on my shoulder for the world, because I didn't know who I was." So, as many struggling kids do, Wesley spent his life trying to fit in. He had no guidance, his self-esteem was low, and no one could see past the façade he put up because of it. "I was very negative, and I was overweight on top of that," he recalls. He was unhealthy and unhappy, believing that no one could get out of the situation he was born into. Wes was surrounded by friends and peers living without any sort of ambition, making just enough to pay bills, doing whatever they had to do—including selling drugs and stealing—to provide for their families. Violence and gunshots ringing out in his neighborhood were everyday occurrences. "You hear about someone getting robbed and be like, 'Alright, man, as long as you're livin'." At the end of the day, it was all about survival.

One night shortly after his 24th birthday, Wes was walking to his car after a disturbance at his ex-girlfriend's home. Seconds after reaching the driver's side, he felt the impact of something he couldn't identify. "I didn't even know what happened. All I knew is that my body tensed up, and something had changed. Everything about my movement, my awareness... I went straight into tunnel vision." He remembers that moment vividly, turning to face a man he didn't recognize, seeing the flash of a gun, and collapsing to the ground. "I didn't feel my body being punctured by a bullet. All I saw was everyone around me start to panic. That's the first thing I noticed," he recalls. "The second thing I noticed was the man running back to his car and getting in it. I'll tell you right now if I wasn't dead from the gunshots, I literally thought I was going to be run over." He remembers the car's tires barely missing his head, and experiencing what people call "your life flashing before your eyes."

"My thought process at that moment was, '*At least I made it to 24...*' Everyone else around me had died or had dealt with someone who'd died from gun violence." He'd lost his first friend at 13, attended about seven funerals a year, and hadn't even expected to live past 21. "I had just gotten sole custody of my daughter three months before my accident. The only thing that was going through my mind is, 'I can't be a father...who's gonna raise my daughter?'"

Next thing Welsey knew, he woke up in the hospital. "I was in ICU, I had a tube down my throat, and I was looking at my family. My mom, my dad, my brothers and sisters—they were just crying. The only thing I *did* know is that I was alive. It hadn't hit me yet that my life had changed forever."

Two weeks later, doctors delivered the devastating news that he had suffered a T11-T12 spinal cord injury, meaning he would be paralyzed from the waist down for the rest of his life.

"I didn't see the point of living," he remembers, "I wondered, '*Why didn't he just finish it?*' This wasn't a life I was willing to accept."

A dark and hopeless time followed, including bedrest for two years and the prospect of facing six surgeries. The 270 pounds he'd carried on his 5' 4" frame caused significant complications with his recovery. "I was heavy, depressed and didn't want to lift my butt up. I sat in my chair every day just drowning in my own sorrows." His home health nurses would have tears in their eyes, heartbroken by his hopelessness and self-hatred. "I would literally beat my legs every day. I was like, '*They don't work anyway!*' Not understanding I was causing more damage for myself."

Eventually, Wesley faced the truth that he still had a little girl to take care of...and that changed everything. "One day, my daughter came in and wanted to push my wheelchair. I said, 'Don't push my wheelchair,' and she said, 'But this is your Superman chair!' And that's probably all it took for me to understand that I had to be Superman for this little girl."

So, how did he do it?

"Well, I quit making excuses. Now, one of my biggest quotes is, 'What do you do when those excuses don't make sense anymore?'" Up to that point, he'd given countless reasons why life in a wheelchair wasn't going to work for him. Then, there was his daughter, who didn't even see it as a disability. So he decided, "Instead of worrying about how the world sees me, why not just focus on how this little girl sees me? And that was all the strength I needed."

He went to the doctor and asked what he could do to change the trajectory of his life. The doctor's unexpected answer: "Add more protein to your diet."

"I was determined to understand what protein was…I thought I got enough protein from McDonalds' Big Macs and Double Quarter Pounders with cheese," he laughs. Growing up in what's known as a "food desert"—an area with limited access to affordable and nutritious food —Wesley had no idea where to even start with healthy eating.

"So, I actually went to school. I could get out for three hours a day, so I enrolled in Johnson County Community College and took a dietitian course. The moment I opened this book on nutrition, it blew my mind." He learned about sugar, and how the Dr. Pepper and Honey Buns he'd lived on to "calm his nerves" were actually working against him.

Wesley started with some simple healthy steps—replaced sugary drinks with water, changed the foods in his house to a cleaner version—and by his last surgery, which took place three years after he was shot, he was 100 pounds lighter. He'd struggled his whole life just to feel good, and now he felt great, despite his physical limitations. "Losing all this weight, my mindset just shifted. It went from '*what I can't do*' to '*I can do whatever I put my mind to!*'"

Still confined to six weeks of lying in bed to heal from surgery, Wesley developed a grand idea. "I felt so different that I started my non-profit in a hospital bed," he beams. He became passionate about encouraging others to change their minds about their limitations, to embrace being different, and to do more than just survive...but to thrive. His organization, Disabled But Not Really, came to life, and a whole new world opened up.

Fresh out of the hospital, he began travelling around the country to expos. "I had this vision to help people with disabilities become healthy and active." Wesley discovered competitions like wheelchair bodybuilding and adaptive CrossFit; he watched people push themselves far past their mental limits. "When you see a guy with one arm doing something that just blows you away, or someone in your position doing a little bit more than what *you* do, there's no reason to make excuses." Wesley began competing around the country, challenging himself to try new things and pushing past old limits. Determined to share his newfound freedom, the Disabled But Not Really idea became a movement with a mission: "To instill in the underserved 'disabled' community, a physically limitless mindset that breeds courage, confidence, and competence."

Today, Disabled But Not Really's impact in the community extends far beyond those with physical disabilities. Through a program called KChange, they bring volunteers together to distribute water, healthy snacks, and care packages to the homeless throughout the year. Wesley believes strongly in providing good nutrition to everyone. "Has anyone ever thought that if they gave these people something good, they might have the energy to go out and find a job?"

The Distrikc is another local effort—this one impacting Kansas City's Eastside where Wes grew up. It's all about empowering those largely unseen and forgotten communities of color in Kansas City...from the inside. This includes helping kids with skills they didn't learn from their parents, giving them a greater chance for a brighter future.

The organization that began in the mind of a paralyzed man in a hospital bed continues to evolve and extend its reach in true Wesley fashion—far beyond expectations.

An hour-long interview with Wesley for my podcast on October 26, 2019, included a hint about a Netflix show that would soon tell his story. They had just finished recording. He could not share the name at the time, but promised I would find out in the coming months.

The final chapter in the story of Wesley's shooting is perhaps the most moving and inspiring of all. He was eventually able to reveal his Netflix debut; he'd been given an opportunity by the Fab Five on the series *Queer Eye* to meet the man who shot him—and he took it. He remembers the intense mess of emotions he experienced beforehand, and then what he describes as a sense of goodness and "cool vibes" the moment he entered the room. As they sat face to face, Wesley gained a better understanding of why things happened the way they did. The shooter's intention was to protect someone from a perceived danger, something Wes says he would have done if the tables were turned.

When asked if he wanted an apology, Wes replied, "I actually want to tell you 'thank you,' because you gave me the best life I ever had. If it wasn't for you, I wouldn't be doing what I'm doing now." The two men had closure that day, but the story continues as Wes finds new opportunities to share his vibrant way of living with others.

"I'm free," he says, "That's why I'm smiling. I'm mentally free from everything I've limited myself to. I'm liberated." No matter what our situation, that's a message we can each take to heart, and who knows where that newfound freedom will lead us?

④ TRUST

TOP OF THE 4TH

I spent my final two years as a student at the University of Wisconsin interning at WMTV, editing video clips for the nightly sportscasts and accompanying a photographer out in the field to hold a microphone, or even on occasion, ask questions to athletes. As a college kid, I found pure joy in catching a glimpse of my hand in a shot on TV or seeing my highlights air on the news. After two years cutting my teeth in a starter market just out of school, I returned to my old station from 1996 to 1998 to serve as a sports producer, photographer, reporter and anchor for my second job since graduating from the UW.

I can picture numerous trips to Lambeau Field to report on the Packers for training camp and home games. We spent time on campus almost daily with Badger athletics being a top priority, and I spent many of my afternoons and nights following high school sports all over the area. They even called me "The Prep Detective" at one point in reference to Jim Carrey's movie character. But we rarely made the 70-mile drive east to Milwaukee for baseball, instead opting to cover the Brewers from our office in Madison. I remember only one trip…the first Major League Baseball game I covered as a professional between the Cubs and Brewers at County Stadium. I don't know who won or lost or who made the big plays. I have no idea why we even went. I just know the teams involved, the location and the approximate time period based on an occurrence with one star player.

Let's call it 1997-ish and I needed a sound bite for the news. My dream of being on the field during batting practice as a reporter had finally come true, but who would I interview? I didn't know one player personally, but mustered up the courage to approach Mark Grace. That's how I know the game featured the Cubs, because Grace starred for the "Lovable Losers" from 1988 through 2000. As a kid who moved from the suburbs of Philadelphia to the North Shore of Chicago in 1985, I rooted against the Cubs, showing allegiance to my beloved Phillies. Plus, I was like most teenage boys...obnoxious! If most of my friends loved the Cubs, I would take solace in providing a dissenting viewpoint. I knew this much though: Mark Grace had a reputation for being one of the nicest and most fun-loving characters in the game. So, the "mid-twenties-me" introduced myself to the friendly first baseman. I remember *nothing* all these years later except this exchange: "Hi Mark, my name is Joel Goldberg. I'm with the NBC TV affiliate in Madison, Wisconsin. Can I grab you for a second?" Grace stared at me. No...*glared* at me for what felt like a full minute. Maybe it was just a few seconds, but long enough for me to question the words that had just come out of my mouth.

Then he replied while maintaining the scowl. "YOU DON'T TOUCH ME," he barked. He let that sit a little longer as my brain now started to question whether I had chosen the right profession. And then a huge smile broke out on his face. "I'm just messin' with you, kid, how can I help you?" And he used a different verb than "messing," which began with an F and ended with an ING. Crisis averted, but all these years later, I wonder why we so often ask for favors, business or anything else, without building a relationship first.

How often do we receive requests on Linkedin for meetings from random people wanting to sell us something? Happens to me almost every day, and it's a non-starter. I went through all those journalism classes in J-School, and never was taught how to build relationships. Today, I view it as the most important part of my job as a broadcaster and motivational speaker. I wish a Professor Joe Maddon had existed in the classroom. Maddon will forever be known as the man who led the Cubs to a World Championship in 2016, ending the franchise's 108-year drought. He's also one of my favorite managers to talk to in baseball because conversations with him can range from wine to book suggestions to leadership to philosophy. Whenever I have the chance to converse with him, I always learn something new. So, in 2018 I walked into Maddon's office and asked him a simple question. "How do you build trust?"

He said, "Trust, to me, is the residue of building relationships. I think people skip relationship building and just want to have trust arrive, but trust cannot arrive until we develop a relationship." Being the renaissance man that he is, he told me that he and a local artist had just designed a print to sell for charity about that very topic. The image featured a kid writing down a series of words. On top is the phrase "Build Relationships" with an arrow pointing down to "Trust," with another arrow down to "Exchange Ideas," which is underlined. Below that is "Constructive Criticism," and finally at the bottom, the word "Flows." I asked him to explain. "Number one is to build relationships, which then leads to trust, which then leads to the exchange of ideas, which then leads to the ability where constructive criticism flows. Because if we don't get those first three things in order, we cannot be constructively critical or exchange ideas without pushback. If you're going to start a culture, if you just really go by those three steps, you will arrive at that point where you can have a meeting or meetings with a group of people and nobody there is going to try and ameliorate the boss." As he shared his theory, I thought about how this advice could apply to anyone, from the locker room to the boardroom to the break room.

At that point in my career, Maddon's words validated what I had learned the hard way as a young reporter: Put down the camera and microphone, forget the sound bite or interview, and just get to know people. There's no player I ever failed at that more with than Albert Pujols. Pujols broke in as a rookie with the St. Louis Cardinals in 2001 and almost instantly became a superstar. Day after day, week after week, month after month and year after year, I failed to connect with Pujols as he became the best player in the world. My impression of the private slugger was molded by the constant rejection for interview requests. Sometimes he said "yes," but more often than not, he would walk off the field and turn me down, leaving me no postgame guest, as I would hear my producer asking through my earpiece, "Who do you have?"

The answer, embarrassingly, was "No one." I can still feel my heart pounding, waiting for the regular repudiation. Let's just be honest...I didn't like Albert Pujols. I also didn't know him.

In 2007, my seventh year with Pujols, I walked up to him in the visiting clubhouse in Houston and asked a simple question: "Can we talk in private? No camera. It's personal." He agreed, and we walked down to the visiting batting cage. Pujols' family had moved to New York from the Dominican Republic when he was a child, and they eventually settled in Kansas City. I told him I wanted his advice—that I had a job opportunity with the Royals, but no one knew, and I hoped he would keep it private. I asked, "What can you share with me about your hometown of Kansas City?" Pujols replied that he couldn't tell me if the job was better, but that KC was an amazing place to live and raise a family. He promised to keep my secret safe and asked me to keep him updated.

Two weeks later, I shared with Pujols that I had indeed landed the job and would move from St. Louis to Kansas City in 2008. He took me to lunch at a small restaurant in the back of a Puerto Rican grocery store in Milwaukee and I sat in bewilderment as he blessed our food and we talked about family and life. I remember thinking, *"How could I go from disliking this man so much to genuinely enjoying his company?"* He even offered to sell me his KC house. I laughed and replied, "Albert, I don't quite make the same kind of money as you."

Over the years, as Pujols moved on to the Los Angeles Angels, he regularly greeted me with a giant hug when he faced the Royals and asked about my wife and kids. He gave me one-on-one interviews and the kind of access a reporter could only dream of from a superstar. He's one of the greatest players in the history of the game. It took me seven years to learn to build that relationship, and another 10 to make an admission to him: I approached him one day in the visiting clubhouse at Kauffman Stadium and said, "Albert, I have a confession to make." He looked at me with curiosity and then turned a bit red with embarrassment as I said, "You used to scare the living heck out of me." His reply taught me a lesson I now apply every day of my life.

Pujols said, "Everyone wants something from me. Once I trust you, I will do anything for you."

BOTTOM OF THE 4TH

How often do we ask people we don't know for something without first earning their trust or building the relationship? That's the mistake I made with Pujols for so many years.

It's a topic I discussed with author and highly sought-after speaker Simon Sinek in October, 2020. I was asked to interview Sinek for the Helzberg Entrepreneurial Mentorship Program (HEMP) at their HEMP Retreat. Sinek is one of my favorite writers, and I never want to miss any of his pearls of wisdom, so he's one of the few people I receive notifications for when he tweets. Known for his ability to help people find their purpose—or their "why"—his 2010 Ted Talk on the topic has been viewed more than 50 million times.

Sinek reminds me of H&R Block CEO Jeff Jones with his ability to craft memorable messages—the kinds of phrases or sayings that end up on a Post-it Note in my office or a digital file of meaningful quotes on my phone. The first time I met Jones, I quickly wrote down a sentence he uttered that blew my mind: "There's a slippery slope between tradition and irrelevance," he told me.

Sinek has a similar impact on leaders with his powerful statements like, "The cost of leadership is self-interest," or, "Vision is the ability to talk about the future with such clarity, it is as if we are talking about the past." Also: "People don't buy what you do; they buy *why* you do it."

During the 45-minute, virtual one-on-one question-and-answer session in front of the "Hempers," I asked Sinek about trust. "Isaac Stern, the famous violinist said, 'Music is what happens between the notes.' Well, trust is what happens between the meetings," Sinek answered. "It's like friendship. You don't go up to someone and say, 'Will you be my friend?' You can't just go up to someone and tell them, 'Trust me.' It's not an order. It's not a request. It's earned."

Jones became the CEO of H&R Block and experienced that mix of nerves and excitement that comes with a new job or role as he made his first speech to his new associates on October 9, 2017. The former president of Uber and chief marketing officer at Target was taking over an iconic tax company. The task at hand was rewriting the H&R Block story. Doing taxes in the 21st century could not possibly compare to 1955 when Richard and Henry Bloch founded the company.

"There are things about this company that we have to cherish and things about this company we have to change," Jones said. "Be unafraid to challenge all the things that have made us successful."

Along with needing to make Block more effective and relevant to the times, Jones knew a high level of skepticism existed due to the numerous leadership changes that employees had endured in recent years. Who could blame associates for experiencing a *"been there, done that, here we go again"* mentality? "I had people look me in the eye and say, 'With all due respect, I love what you're saying but I've heard it before. I outlasted all the other guys and I'll probably outlast you, too.' I literally had the vice president of the company say that to me." How Jones reacted to such criticism gave early clues to his leadership style. "I thanked him, and I thanked him because he had the courage to tell me what I knew others were thinking."

With phrases like "better together" and "clear roles, common goals," Jones wanted his leadership team to develop a new strategy on its own instead of outsourcing to a third party. Create buy-in and ownership. Do that critical work of listening. In short, he needed to build trust because, let's be honest, most people generally look at the boss as, well...the boss. He needed to be real.

So, who is Jeff Jones?

"A kid from West Virginia who's accomplished more than most people thought he could, given where he came from, but a guy who thinks he's just getting started," Jones told me.

He started hosting regular coffee meetings with different company directors, just to chat about anything. He also began eating in the H&R Block cafeteria, pulling up a seat and introducing himself to strangers. That only became awkward when he learned the cafeteria was open to the public and he realized he was meeting non-employees. But hey, even visitors learned about the man without needing to know he was the chief executive officer.

"I like to be Jeff before I like to be CEO," said Jones. "I just have a really deep belief that people do their best when they know the truth. People are people. They like to relate to each other. People like to understand that I'm a dad, I'm a husband, I like to play golf, I like music. And so, I think the more people that get to know me, and the more I demonstrate who I am...the more they listen to me and want to buy into ideas when I'm asking them to do hard things."

The music interests of Jones, who's in his fifties, include Justin Timberlake... but mostly because of his one interaction with the powerhouse performer. This is where the "people are people" observation applies. It's so easy to put highly accomplished individuals on pedestals, but Jones would so much rather be treated like everyone else. It's exactly what I missed with Pujols early on. It's a skill Jones put to use with Timberlake. Set to speak in front of thousands of Target employees at the Target Center arena in

Minneapolis, he donned the standard attire—a red Target shirt and khakis. The company had worked on a campaign with Timberlake, and he would be there. Jones walked in to meet the musician and Timberlake greeted him with a memorable observation: "Damn, you look good."

That was Jeff's JT experience. But there was more, and it came down to what I believe is a quick version of trust building. Jones could have acted like a crazed fan and been in awe of the iconic superstar, maybe dropping an awkward "SexyBack" song reference. But he chose to treat him like a normal guy and brought up an interest he knew they shared. Jones and Timberlake talked about golf. "People are people. They like to be related to, and that's what I tried to do," he said.

What he did with Timberlake that day is what I do when looking to build trust at a moment's notice. When I need a quick comment or interview with a superstar that I haven't met, I try to find a common bond that can take away the awkwardness of not knowing them. But what about long-term trust? Jones knew he needed to think big at Block.

The new CEO thought about goals. What was he trying to do? He described it this way: At the highest level, he wanted to build growth. To grow, you need to innovate. What's one of the keys to innovation? Speed—going faster and learning faster. How does a group successfully move fast? By establishing shorthand with each other. Jones explains "shorthand" as the knowledge and feelings colleagues share that enable them to complete each other's sentences or move in a certain direction without having to say it. In sports terms, it's the chemistry or rhythm athletes get in when they find a groove. My own daily experience with my longtime broadcast partner Jeff Montgomery is similar. After thousands of shows over the years, I spend zero time or energy wondering how he will react or handle any situation. I just know he will deliver in the same way a star quarterback trusts that his favorite receiver in football will be where he's supposed to be. That's what Jones calls shorthand—allowing you to get there faster. What do you need to create shorthand in your world? It all starts with trust.

Remember what Sinek said about building friendships? Jones offered a similar thought: "I try to approach the business of trust building like any relationship...with a child, with a friend, with a spouse. The first thing that I've always tried to role-model is this idea that you have to *give* to *get*. You've got to put yourself out there first. You've got to demonstrate vulnerability and authenticity first, and when you start doing that, then people understand that your motivations are pure." These are the foundational building blocks of trust that lead to a higher level where teaching can occur, and expectations among a team will grow.

Back in 2017, Jones believed if he and his team could create the right atmosphere and synergy at Block, they could take the company to where it needed to be. He knew they should honor the past and learn from it. But it was time to move forward. "When you work for an iconic, historic company, or you have family traditions, or you belong to an organization that has a lot of history, you can run into trouble if what you do is spend all your time celebrating the past," Jones told me. "In today's world, you see companies especially that were thriving yesterday, and today are literally gone."

Think about the emergence of Netflix and the disappearance of Blockbuster, or the evolution of people preferring Uber instead of taxi cabs. Jones saw a new future for the recognizable but out-of-touch brand. So, he sought to build the ultimate platform to enable any American to access taxes on their terms, as easily as possible.

Three years after joining H&R Block as its CEO, Jones is thrilled with the progress. "Never done, but definitely headed in the right direction." The same can be said about moving forward during the pandemic, a period Jones navigated like every other leader.

He sums it up well: "Trust has never been more important in a world where no one knows the truth."

5 FACE-TO-FACE

TOP OF THE 5TH

On March 3, 2017, I began a critical new practice in my life—something that started at Corner Bakery in the Kansas City suburb of Leawood, Kansas, and continues to this day. Networking! Yes, I finally understood after all those years that I needed to take my locker room mingling skills to the business world. I kicked it off with what would be the first of many coffee meetings with Steve Johns, a man who would come to have a significant impact on my life. Steve had been a long-time attorney and executive for a large organization responsible for mergers, acquisitions and building businesses. Today, he's president and CEO of the Heartland Heroes, a peer group of entrepreneurs, business owners and chief executive officers. (And a group I'm now a part of!)

From that day forward, face-to-face coffees, breakfasts, lunches and happy hours became routine (especially during my baseball off-seasons) as I built a network from scratch. Sometimes I'd have three, four or five in a day, almost always kicking off in the morning with coffee. I tried to absorb like a sponge, learning so much about all kinds of people, soaking up every bit of advice about business and speaking that I could obtain. Hundreds and hundreds of connections, some occasionally leading to business opportunities, but almost all resulting in improving my knowledge outside the world of broadcasting. Over time, I found myself offering my own perspective to others and paying it forward.

The power of human interaction can never be underestimated, and that continued to show itself during a pandemic...just in digital form. It's a Small Ball tip that is easy to dismiss as our schedules just seem to get fuller and technology offers more convenient, less time-consuming options for "connecting." But being in the presence of another person is an irreplaceable experience. Whether in a coffee shop, restaurant, or even on a home visit, there's so much more we can learn about a person beyond a resume, LinkedIn profile or scouting report. And if that means spending time on a Zoom call with coffee or drinks, there's still an opportunity to get to know someone.

Alana Muller, a former executive turned business coach, networking speaker and workshop facilitator, is the author of the book, *Coffee Lunch Coffee: A Practical Field Guide for Master Networking.* She's the master at making connections and said, "For me, Small Ball is every single relationship. Every single one. You simply don't know how you're going to interact with one another. How you're going to change one another's lives. How you're going to add value for one another over the course of time." She talked about how she had once invited 205 people to meet with her over a nine-month period of time, and 200 said "yes." This success was the result of early intentionality. Not necessarily to land more business, but to open doors...and those 200 connections led to professional, community and social opportunities over time.

This has been my exact experience with André Davis, whom I clicked with instantly. André works in business development for a construction company, and it often takes multiple meetings with someone before he even talks about himself. The key, I learned from

André, was to try to spend more time listening and learning at these meetings. André and I spent well over an hour and a half during our first coffee, and I immediately wanted to set up another. I know we will work together on different projects in the future. I don't know what those might be, but we align over values and the connection feels right. I want to work with people like André Davis.

I shared a similar experience with Diego Gutierrez when we first sat down in 2019 as I quickly discovered that Diego is a guy who never sits still...something I can totally relate to, and just one of many things we have in common. We both work too hard and could afford to take a break every now and then! We were both born in 1972; both grew up loving and playing soccer; both became broadcasters...but the comparison ends there with his elite soccer skills and discipline in the classroom far exceeding mine.

Diego had one goal as a kid: to become a professional soccer player. Growing up in the country of Colombia, he ate, drank and slept soccer, developing into a prodigy by playing with older kids. But by his mid-teens, his father's family business was falling apart. His mother, who had family in America, didn't ask him...she *told* him that he would put soccer on hold and go study in the States as a 17-year-old. He didn't know much English but was determined to succeed in school *and* his beloved sport, and he became one of the top soccer recruits in the U.S., landing at Evansville University which, at the time, had the top program in the country.

Diego admits that upon his arrival in Evansville his English was good enough to understand, but not sufficient to learn what he needed to learn in school. Add in the cultural element of an immigrant kid submersed in Southern Indiana with no one speaking his primary language, and he found himself in an extremely uncomfortable situation. The kid who would one day become a college professor was barricading himself in his dorm room, improving his English by watching Sports Center anchors Dan Patrick and Keith Olbermann on ESPN. He went on to play professionally for the Kansas City Wizards and the Chicago Fire. He also became an American citizen and a member of the U.S. National Soccer Team.

Diego understood that the ball would someday stop rolling after his soccer career and he'd need a second life. He explored the scouting and front office side of soccer but felt unfulfilled, so he found another path—the Helzberg School of Business in Kansas City, where he received his MBA in 2014, then Creighton University for his Doctor of Business Administration in 2015. He became an associate professor teaching graduate classes at Rockhurst University in business and marketing.

Diego truly values human connection and has always been a person who loves helping others. His playing career gave him a massive platform, so he assisted Major League Soccer in starting its charitable arm, was a representative for the United Nations, and is now in the World Humanitarian Hall of Fame—one of just two soccer players. (The other is the legendary Pelé.) He brought the same energy he displayed on the soccer pitch to the classroom. "One of the reasons I love this profession is that I get to interact with younger people; I get to help develop someone," he said.

Diego also seeks connection through one of his other loves: coffee (another thing we have in common!) "I love drinking coffee, but I think more than anything I love what coffee represents. A cup of coffee is a union. It's community with somebody. It's a time to reflect, sometimes a time to love, a time to heal. So many things that I'm able to do with a cup of coffee in my hand. Life has got so many of these little miracles that pop up every now and then." He said he finds comfort, peace and symbolism in a cup of coffee.

These days, when he's not teaching or spending time with his family, he's playing golf, working on numerous projects and serving as a soccer broadcaster on Spanish radio. While the pandemic of 2020 put a halt to our in-person coffees, we hit the golf course one afternoon instead, continuing our discussions at a safe distance outdoors.

Whether it's coffee, lunch or a Zoom call, there's always so much to learn from a face-to-face meeting.

BOTTOM OF THE 5TH

People often ask me who my favorite player of all time to interview is, and it's an impossible question to answer. But I *can* say the best, most consistent go-to guy in my career has been Eric Hosmer, a first baseman who said "yes" to every request of mine over the years except one (more on that in a bit).

In the fall of 2007, Hosmer played on an elite high school tournament team in Jupiter, Florida sponsored by the Atlanta Braves. One of the coaches of Hosmer's team, Lonnie Goldberg (no relation to me), worked for the Braves in the scouting department.

"Me and Lonnie hit it off big time in that tournament. I think we were sitting next to each other every single game," Hosmer, now in his thirties, recalled about those early years. The Royals hired Goldberg as director of baseball operations about a month after the tournament, and a light bulb went on for Hosmer when he realized Kansas City held the third pick in the upcoming 2008 amateur draft. He remembers thinking, "There's no way this guy is not going to take me. If he's got any seniority or any rank when it comes to that pick, then I think I'm going to the Royals for sure."

Fortunately, Royals GM Dayton Moore encouraged opinions and feedback from all members of his baseball operations staff, including newcomers. Goldberg admits, "I was biased," but he fully believed Eric Hosmer to be the sure pick."

Organizations spend years watching high school and college players. The Royals followed numerous prospects, including Eric Hosmer, prior to the 2008 draft. They observed every one of his high school games leading up to the draft with multiple sets of eyes on him. But as often happens in business, the scouting reports and the stats don't always reveal the full picture. Goldberg knew Hosmer as the kid from the tournament in Jupiter, but he also saw a potential star who could become a transformative piece for his new organization. "When the best player on the team is the hardest worker and best teammate, you have a chance to be real special," he recalled.

At Goldberg's nudging, Dayton Moore and Assistant GM J.J. Picollo made a visit to the Hosmer house in South Florida a week before the draft. Picollo still remembers the way the young player presented himself and the fact that it was very clear he'd been raised the right way, in a loving family: "We walked out of there thinking that this guy could be the face of the franchise...well-spoken, well-grounded, not intimidated by the conversation, answered questions directly. All the things you look for in people, but especially when you are talking about an 18-year-old."

Typically, when choosing between an elite high school player and a safer-bet college player, the college kids will show better due to their classroom experiences and exposure to the media. But Hosmer checked all those boxes at a younger age. Growing up, he had always played with the older kids.

Picollo continued: "Those meetings are really important because you're making million-dollar investments, and who gets hired for a job without ever going for a job interview?" On the diamond, Hosmer carried himself as a leader: "What you saw on the field, you saw in his house," Picollo said.

What Moore and Picollo observed that day included Hosmer's dad, Mike, and his mom, Ileana. Hosmer can talk about any subject eloquently, but his parents are at the top of his list: "My dad showed me work ethic, being a firefighter, coming home after a 48-hour shift. Me and my brother being right there at the door and him never saying 'no,'" Hosmer recalls, beaming with pride in his voice. Ileana, the oldest of seven children, had come to the United States from Cuba as a seven-year-old. She was the rock of a large family as a child.

Her brother, Joey, the fifth of the seven Someillan children, remembers his parents having to learn a new language and work very hard. According to Joey, Illeana "was our second mom as a teenager. She helped raise all of us."

Eric's childhood memories echo that of his Uncle Joey's. "My mom just always had a way to relate to everybody…she had the respect from everybody, and she did it in such a cool, calm way." Funny, because during his seven-year tenure with the Royals, Hoz (as we always call him) could be described with the same work ethic as Mike and the same ability to relate to all people like Ileana.

Hosmer connected with everyone regardless of background, race or language. His longtime manager Ned Yost saw Hoz's on-and-off-the-field abilities right away. "He was a very mature young man. He was a very self-confident young man, and not in a disgusting way," Yost told me. Translation: Hosmer was "the man" without acting like he was better than everyone else. Yost, now retired, reflected on Hosmer by using the analogy of an invisible stamp that can't be seen by the naked eye: "He had "leader" on his forehead written in that ink. You had to have the light to see it, but if you could see it, it showed bright."

Pick any characteristic of a top leader, and Hosmer fits the bill. Confident? Absolutely. Humble? Every day. Empathetic? He always listened and cared. Accountable? I watched it first-hand. Trailing 6-4 in the seventh inning on May 9, 2017 against the Tampa Bay Rays in St. Petersburg, Florida, Hosmer hit a two-out single. Catcher Salvador Perez stepped up to the plate with Hosmer on first, and center fielder Lorenzo Cain on second base. A hit could've tied the game, but Hosmer was picked off first by the pitcher to end the rally. I remember thinking that such a blunder could be costly, but the Royals later mounted a comeback and won in extra innings. Still, the media approached Hosmer after the game and asked about the base running mishap. He took full responsibility for making a mistake and credited his teammates for taking him off the hook. Later that evening, I sat outside at the hotel with Hoz and his family for a drink. Off the clock, I would not ask about the game. This was social. But Uncle Joey needed no such filter, and asked his nephew, "Hey Eric, what happened on that play at first?" Hosmer proceeded to explain that after getting tagged out, first-base coach Rusty Kuntz said he had misread the pitcher and apologized to Hosmer for messing up the play. I sat there listening to the story and thinking about how confident a player must be to take the blame for another's mistake. Also, what it must have felt like for the coach to see the star player have his back. No one ever knew. Eric Hosmer was always accountable to his teammates.

Hosmer blew me off once. Only once. A few months after the pickoff at first, he was batting in the ninth inning at Kauffman Stadium. Two runners on, two outs, Colorado led 4-3. Hosmer homered in dramatic fashion to win the game. The crowd went crazy. His

Photo Courtesy: John Sleezer, Kansas City

teammates mobbed him as he crossed home plate in what turned into a mosh pit of excitement. I prepared to interview him as the star of the game in front of the crowd and the audience at home on live TV. This would be a slam dunk! Except Royals Vice President of Media Relations Mike Swanson informed me that Hosmer declined. Something about his shirt being ripped off in the celebration. I was stunned. It didn't add up.

Hoz never said "no" to me or to "Swanee," one of the top media relations executives in baseball.

I received a text just a few minutes later while hosting our postgame show. It was Hosmer. "Dude, don't be upset. I couldn't do it without a shirt." A player texting so quickly after the game was not normal, especially after declining to do an interview. I didn't buy the shirt story, but quickly realized the likely reason for Hosmer's denial. He had hit the home run off Rockies closer Greg Holland, Hosmer's longtime former teammate and fellow 2015 World Champion. I suspected that he just didn't want to gloat in front of someone he viewed as a brother.

Hosmer fessed up to me one October day in 2020. "Kansas City's going crazy, and he's just there walking off…I didn't want to go and really talk about it on TV and keep putting salt in the wound." The celebration at the plate was enough. He admitted to me that someone had to be disrespected in that moment, but he had hoped that texting me immediately to essentially say "no hard feelings or bad intent meant" would show me a sign of respect. That's exactly how I felt, and had always suspected it was Hoz, just taking care of Holland.

I was chatting with iconic Boston Red Sox superstar and three-time world champion David "Big Papi" Ortiz on September 12, 2014, two Fridays before the Royals would clinch their first playoff berth in 29 years. He told me he gave the Royals players encouragement as they knocked on the door of the postseason. "This city needs you guys to take them to the playoffs. If you make that happen, you guys are going to make history for this city." That message, and Papi's vision turned out to be prophetic. A city became transfixed by this Cinderella squad as the Royals won their first eight postseason games that year, the first MLB team to ever accomplish such a feat.

Following the unexpected sweep of the Los Angeles Angels in three games (one former player-turned-television-pundit called the Royals a "cute story" and predicted L.A. would win every game), Eric Hosmer and teammates Johnny Giavotella and Jarrod Dyson decided to celebrate at McFadden's Sports Saloon, a short 13 miles from Kauffman Stadium. Hosmer sent out a tweet before leaving the locker room that read, "KC you guys showed us so much love all year we're returning the favor for you guys tonight at @McFaddensKC #allonebigfamily see.u all there."

About an hour later, the trio arrived at the saloon in Kansas City's Power and Light district, greeted by the police. "You don't understand what you just created," Hosmer remembers hearing from the cops. Thousands of fans had gathered yelling, screaming, wanting a glimpse of the local heroes. "People were banging on the windows and we are like, 'This is incredible!'" Hosmer, Dyson and Giavotella decided to show their appreciation. They threw down a credit card and bought free drinks for every fan in attendance for an hour, tallying a bar tab somewhere in the $15,000 to $20,000 range, with ringleader Hosmer blazing the trail and cementing an already legendary status as the face of the franchise.

A lot of fans who were there that night could vouch for the observation Lonnie Goldberg made back at that high school baseball tournament about a teenager who was about to be given a $6 million signing bonus: "The guy that everyone wanted to be around, the guy that during the rain delay, everyone was sitting around was Hoz. It didn't matter what nationality. Eric was different." True in 2007, still the case in 2014, and once again in 2020, when he helped the dormant San Diego Padres return to the postseason for the first time since 2006, in just his third year with them.

To this day Hosmer stands out as the best leader I've covered in baseball. Stats and numbers show some of the picture, but there's always more to the story...often best told face to face.

⑥ ATTENTION TO DETAIL

TOP OF THE 6TH

I remember attending a Kansas City Business Journal event one evening and listening to four impressive guests on stage. They all imparted bits of wisdom and commanded the attention of the audience, but one particular impression remains with me to this day. The highest profile guest on the panel was Sandy Kemper. Now that I know him, I know he would humbly disagree with my assessment, most likely offering a self-deprecating reason for his top billing: "I might've been older than all of them put together."

Alexander "Sandy" Kemper comes from a well-known Kansas City banking family whose name is plastered on buildings all over town. Look at Sandy and you would never guess it. He's the guy showing up to work in Wrangler jeans and boots and bringing fresh vegetables and meat for his employees from his farm.

I had never met Sandy but found myself mesmerized by his attention to detail that day. Not in his responses to the moderator, but in his actions toward his fellow panelists. Kemper spent every moment on stage furiously taking notes in his journal when the other experts answered questions. I kept thinking, *"Here's this man who's one of the most successful and biggest name businessmen and philanthropists in town, and he's locked in on every moment, attempting to learn."* I needed to invite this intriguing leader on my podcast and find out what made him tick. Why so precise with the journal?

My arrival to the C2FO offices weeks later to record that podcast took place on the day after the company celebrated hitting $100 billion of funding to customers around the world. Kemper's company had grown to nearly 500 employees worldwide. He's been referred to as a twin or a body double to the iconic Mr. Clean character made famous in commercials for generations. If you had never met Kemper or known about the Mr. Clean look, you would struggle to pick him out in the company's Leawood, Kansas headquarters. Mixed in with his staff in a large open space with standing desks and white board walls, Kemper ditches his large CEO corner office (if he even has one) to be a piece of the puzzle, not the star of the show. "I love the team the most," Kemper said. So... what about that journal? More on that and Kemper's note-taking ritual in a bit.

Kemper founded C2FO, an early payment platform, in 2008. Within 10 years, it reached a valuation of more than $1 billion. C2FO's mission is to create a future where every company around the world has the capital needed to grow. Put simply, C2FO unlocks a company's trapped cash, eliminating their reliance on traditional financing and lending.

As we started the podcast, we discussed one of my favorite topics. His thought on it: "Everyone says strategy eats tactics for breakfast. But culture eats strategy every moment of the day. If you don't have your culture right, it doesn't matter one bit how great your strategy or tactics are," Kemper said.

I told him I've always felt like sports teams that build and sustain a culture could add the word "Way" next to their name—The Yankees Way, The Cardinals Way, The Patriots Way (enter Deflategate comment here if you so choose). Kemper agreed, but also pushed back on the idea of there being just one way. At C2FO, with offices and employees located around the world, Kemper and his leadership team must pay attention to the details needed to keep employees from 180 countries with different cultures connected. "There are nuances to the various countries where we operate. The India C2FO Way is different than the United States C2FO Way is different than the UK C2FO Way." The details that matter most, according to Kemper, are fundamentals, transparency, respect for each other, company before team, and team before self.

"Almost every time that we have an occasion to talk as a company... there is an element of culture to it. There's a learning that we want to bring...not just for the new folks that are coming in, but for some of the old folks as well. Those cultural touchstones that we have are so fundamentally important that we study them and try to articulate them. It is not dissimilar to the way stories were passed along in tribes of men and women back in the early days of human society. We try to remember the songs that were sung around the campfire no matter whether we are around the campfire or London or Shanghai or Mumbai or Delhi."

He continued, "As long as we have those campfires, as long as something is being sung, we don't care if it's a different language, different tone. We want there first and foremost to be campfires, and then we want to make sure that someone is singing it around them, commentating what it is and why we do it. Then, we can add their own vernacular to it. But the fundamental goal is there are campfires and people gathering and stories being told, and that's what influences and...continues your culture."

So why the journal?

"Learning is hard. Learning is a discipline. You have to have the discipline and that drive to learn because I think everybody wants to learn. They're curious and they have that desire, but sometimes 10 years in, 15 years in, 20 years in, it can be hard," Kemper said.

"For me, the notebook is my mental cue, my reminder that I should be paying attention and learning. So the act of taking out the book is a forcing act for me to really pay attention...I could've been thinking about the answer I wanted to give next; I could've been wondering about the next question that was going to be asked."

It's one thing to write down endless observations, but then what? At the end of the week, Kemper looks back at his notes on Saturday morning at home over a cup of coffee. He reviews notes from every meeting, each entry from his journal, and all the internal company reports for a couple of hours before his kids wake up. Sandy said he probably should review the journal every day, but the discipline in committing his Saturday mornings to this process keeps him grounded.

A review of his journal can dig up some gems that provide insight into life and business. For example, Kemper mentioned an entry that he wrote from someone asking the question, "What's the best advice you could give a parent?"

And the response was, "To remember what it was like to be a kid." This insight serves as a reminder that some of C2FO's startup offices in places like India and China with a dozen or so employees are in the same spot Sandy and his then-smaller Kansas crew occupied as up-and-comers nine years ago. The result being grace, courtesy and empathy.

There were so many powerful takeaways from a 45-minute podcast with Kemper, including this gem for all the hopeful dreamers and entrepreneurs in search of the secret sauce: "I know how little I don't know, and I also know that there's no one silver bullet for anything. I've seen people take paths that are diametrically opposed to what I thought they should do and be wonderfully successful." But he told me that focusing on five words can help any aspiring entrepreneur: Curiosity, empathy, passion, intellect and tenacity. He said curiosity tops the list. "If you can't maintain that fire for curiosity, understanding the *why* of the things you're studying—if you can't get that, you're going to have a hard time being successful in your endeavors."

My March 10, 2020 visit included a handshake and a heavy dose of hand sanitizer. The world as we knew it, pre-shutdown, would soon change as employers began the challenging task of sending employees home due to the dangers of the Covid-19 virus. C2FO made the transition easier than others, having conducted a dress rehearsal in early March.

Sandy Kemper led the charge, paying attention to detail every step of the way.

BOTTOM OF THE 6TH

Ask anyone who the star of the 1984 MLB World Champions Detroit Tigers was, and the answers will vary. Lou Whitaker, Lance Parrish and Chet Lemon all started for the American League All-Star team that year. Future Hall of Famers Jack Morris and Alan Trammell played prominent roles. Willie Hernandez won the Cy Young award and was named the Most Valuable Player of the league, and local product Kirk Gibson finished in the top 10 of MVP voting.

A 29-year-old outfielder named Rusty Kuntz played in 84 games during the regular season, notching 40 hits and two home runs. He came to the plate just three times during the Tigers' magical postseason run. He's remembered to this day in the Motor City for his plate appearance on October 14, 1984. Kuntz could hardly believe the directive from legendary manager Sparky Anderson. During game five of the World Series—a tie game with San Diego—Anderson told him to grab a bat. Rusty's reply was simply, "Why?"

Kuntz swung at the first pitch and popped up a blooper beyond the infield dirt in right field. His body language represented that of a player who'd just failed with the bases loaded. However, Gibson, the base runner at third, made a gutsy sprint home and scored on the shallow sacrifice fly. Kuntz found his way into the history books, credited for knocking in the winning run of the Tigers World Series clinching game. There's a lesson here: Every role matters, and anyone on the team can be called upon at any moment. (More on the topic of roles in Chapter 11.)

As for the man who asked "why," Kuntz continued to ask that question well into the 21st century as a coach. Curious and interested in always digging deeper, Rusty Kuntz has become a Yoda of sorts in baseball. With his Robert Redford mop of blond hair and loud, high-pitched voice, he's known for his universal greeting of "Player," which he calls almost anyone he comes into contact with. He's a sage expert with a lifetime's worth of knowledge. So I turned the tables on him one fall day in 2020 at the stadium. I heard the familiar "What's up, Player?" as I approached him. I asked Rusty if he'd always had the desire to search for more information. "I guess I wanted to know *why* all the time," he answered. It's not enough in Rusty's eyes to just take batting practice every day. It's not just about baseball. It might be how the groundskeeper waters the infield. Whatever stops him and catches his attention, or makes his mind wander and wonder, finds its way to an ongoing list he compiles.

As Rusty became a respected coach, thanks to his healthy curiosity, he wanted to know the reason for daily activities. He recalled his own years of preparation as a player. In those days, "I just had to worry about me and what it took for *me* to get ready." But as a coach, "It wasn't about me. It was about how to get other players better. And I have a memory that is about five seconds, so I had to start to write things down. I would think of something and two minutes later, it would be gone." Kuntz said.

He believes there are eight elements that need teaching in baseball: Hitting, catching, pitching, infield, bunting, outfield, base running and base stealing. He specializes in the last four. Rusty began coaching professional baseball in 1987, and has spent the better part of five decades teaching and sharing his expertise while serving in multiple roles, with the bulk of his time spent as a first-base coach. "I didn't just want to be a coach, I wanted to be a difference." But with modest career playing numbers—to put it kindly—he understood he needed to prove his worth to players who carried a natural skepticism of their young coach. "Of course they can Google anything and they said, 'How can you tell *me* how to steal a base when you had five in your whole career?'"

How in-depth does Kuntz's mind go with the details? Try taking his 76-question outfield quiz. Some sample questions include:

There are no runners on base. Ground ball is hit down either line or in the gap. Does the outfielder look or not look at the base runner before making his throw to second base?

How many times do you say "I got it" on a fly ball?

A sinking line drive is hit at you. What part of your body determines whether you catch the ball with the glove up or the glove down?

When managing a throw quickly, do you take your hand to the glove or the glove to your hand?

(Answers at the end of the chapter.)

Baseball coaches generally live in a different world than the average nine-to-fiver, arriving at the ballpark early in the afternoon for an evening game and logging nonstop hours of preparation at home, in hotel rooms, on planes and at the stadium. I remember asking Rusty once, following a much-needed off day in the Bay Area, what he did to occupy his time. I told him I wandered San Francisco for hours. It's one of the best cities to explore on a day off. Rusty expressed shock at my commitment to relax, and told me he spent the day ordering room service and watching video of the team's next opponent. His thirst for knowledge and desire to uncover the tiniest of details make him a commodity to any organization. He wakes up every morning with a goal of finding 10 new things he hasn't seen, heard or done before, and then he adds them to his list.

Kuntz maintains the same work ethic in spring training, only earlier. He wakes up every day at 4:30 a.m. and starts writing on a notepad by his hotel bed. *How can he help a certain player improve? What creative drill might break up the monotony?* After completing this pre-dawn ritual, he heads to the team's facility around 5 a.m. and returns to his room in the early evening. Day after day. "You just pass out, go to sleep, wake up in the middle of the night, write some more stuff down, get up and do it all over again." Simply put, he said, "If you're not putting in 14-16 hours, you're getting cheated." Rusty talks about this without a hint of complaint or dread. He loves it. This man truly lives baseball and he's always the most energetic person in the dugout and on the field. Not bad for a guy who turned 65 years old in 2020. "Ohhhhh, Player!"

"So wait, a first-base coach doesn't just tell a player to go to second or stay put?" I asked Kuntz in jest. He smiled at that common question and began talking animatedly about the art of base running, secondary shuffles, delayed steals, and bodies in motion.

How can I best describe his passion for base running and stealing? Let's go back to those countless hours of searching for details…a process that includes scouring video of the opponent's pitchers and searching for a key from anyone who may step on a mound. Translation: He's looking for a tell in the same way a poker player searches for a bluff. Perhaps a subtle movement of the body, a twitch of the glove or facial expression that may foreshadow a pitcher throwing home versus making a pickoff move to first base. I asked Rusty how long he spends per game day in the video room digging for those keys. He laughed in a way that suggested pure joy in this tedious task, and guessed four to five hours a day. Sometimes finding that key can take days. If he finds it, he's unlocked the base stealing game that may lead to a win. He once saw something from an opponent early in the year that enabled the Royals to steal 19 bases in a season against that opponent. It's like finding a needle in a haystack, but Rusty lives for the search. Asked if he loves it, he replied, "Ohhhh yeah, it's gold."

He often holds court discussing the intricacies of baseball, sharing his creative thoughts for as long as an audience will listen. I can say with certainty that I've learned more about the details of the game from Rusty Kuntz than anyone in my career. Countless players, coaches, managers and broadcasters feel the same.

As for those questions...

There are no runners on base. Ground ball is hit down either line or in the gap. Does the outfielder look or not look at the base runner before making his throw to second base?

Answer: Not look

How many times do you say "I got it" on a fly ball?

Answer: Until you make the catch.

A sinking line drive is hit at you. What part of your body determines whether you catch the ball with the glove up or the glove down?

Answer: Your waist

When managing a throw quickly, do you take your hand to the glove or the glove to your hand?

Answer: Hand to glove

Rusty Kuntz ends the outfield quiz with one bonus question:

Bases loaded. Ground ball hit to the outfield and a "pig" runs out on the field and swallows the ball. What's the ruling on the field?

Answer: Inside the pork home run

Did I mention his attention to detail also includes a sense of humor?

⑦ HIT THE CURVE

TOP OF THE 7TH

Alex Gordon took the field for practice in Lincoln on a June day in 2005 as his University of Nebraska Huskers prepared for a Super Regional playoff matchup against the University of Miami and future big leaguers Ryan Braun and Jon Jay. Gordon's older brother, Eric, sat in the stands, tasked with monitoring Major League Baseball's amateur draft. Alex expected to be selected in the top 10...perhaps even the first five. He had told his brother to send a signal and hold up the corresponding number of fingers to his draft position.

"I thought it was going to be three fingers, which would have been Seattle," Gordon told me. He had communicated more with the Mariners leading up to the draft, but he never made it to the third slot. Alex saw Eric hold up two fingers, meaning the Royals were selecting the third baseman. "So, when it was Kansas City, I wasn't expecting it. I was kind of thrown off a little bit, but I couldn't have been more excited or blown away by just growing up so close to it."

Alex grew up in Lincoln, Nebraska, and his family made the three-hour drive to Kansas City every summer for visits to Worlds of Fun amusement park and to Kauffman Stadium for Royals games. "I remember sitting up in the nosebleeds, third deck, and just watching games," he recalls. Alex's favorite player in the league was Ken Griffey, Jr., because of the ease of how he swung the bat. Gordon would one day meet him, speechless and in awe.

The Gordons also loved to see Royals star George Brett play and interestingly enough, as Alex joined the team all those years later, fans and the media compared him to Brett from the beginning. There was no avoiding the pressure. The next George Brett tasked with turning around the fate of a struggling franchise, which just happened to be his boyhood team.

Alex skyrocketed through the minor league system and reached the big leagues less than two years after being drafted. He made his Royals debut April 2, 2007, on opening day in Kansas City. Designated hitter Mike Sweeney's first-inning single loaded the bases and the crowd of 41,257 broke into a standing ovation—not for the three straight Royals hits, but for Alex Gordon, the prospect who was stepping into the batter's box for the first time. His parents and brothers had once again convened at Kauffman Stadium, this time to watch their own. His fiancée, Jamie, also attended. Red Sox superstar pitcher Curt Schilling stood on the mound and Gordon admits he felt a bit intimidated. He battled and faced six pitches before Schilling struck him out with a nasty split finger fastball. Gordon walked back to the first-base dugout, and the crowd stood again for another ovation. This was day one of support on a journey that would last 14 seasons but take an unexpected path...because how often does the journey go as planned? We are constantly being thrown curveballs in life.

Gordon played well enough in 2007 and 2008. Injuries derailed much of his 2009 and he returned from hip surgery in July, a 25-year-old player out of rhythm and lacking confidence. His struggles continued in 2010 and he was called into manager Trey Hillman's office in the visiting clubhouse in St. Petersburg, Florida on May 1, following a game against the Tampa Bay Rays where Gordon played sparingly. He was hitting a paltry .194 with one home run. General Manager Dayton Moore also sat in the office and did most of the talking. They wanted Alex to return to the minor leagues and change positions. The team had a young third-base prospect waiting in the wings and thought a change of roles might suit Gordon. "I was a little ticked off by it at the time, but at the same time I knew I was struggling so I knew this might be an opportunity to maybe just take a step back, take a deep breath, kind of make an adjustment," he said.

He respected Moore and responded with a "yes, sir" acknowledgment. Gordon joined the Omaha Royals May 4, batting third and playing in left field. The pressure followed him to the Royals Triple-A franchise because his transformation would be taking place just 60 miles from home under a massive magnifying glass. Proud Nebraskans viewed Gordon as a second son.

But he locked in, relying on his greatest attribute—hard work. He immediately connected with Rusty Kuntz, the Royals first-base coach in previous years who had taken on a role as a minor league outfield instructor (and later returned to coach first in 2012). He told Kuntz, "Don't sugarcoat anything." Gordon wanted to learn and move back up without being a defensive liability. He would become Kuntz's greatest pupil and the two worked hand-in-hand, including many years at the big-league level.

I remember taking my wife and young kids to Omaha on a Royals off-day that summer to visit the zoo and watch the Triple-A team play. We sat behind home plate, chatting with Alex's wife Jamie, who was pregnant with the Gordons' first child. Ten years later and now the father of three, Gordon credits Kuntz, then Omaha Manager Mike Jirschele and his staff, and his wife for a remarkable turnaround. Gordon, never one to show a look of panic, admits he felt the pressure with fatherhood looming and a career potentially on the ropes.

"Jamie was there with me from day one of that…I was never reaching out for people trying to feel sorry for me or anything like that. She knew that I needed some pick-me-up every once in a while."

He returned to the majors July 23 with a new manager. Ned Yost had replaced Hillman during Gordon's time away. Set to face the Yankees, Gordon was called into Yost's office in the Bronx. "He was like, 'Hey kid, I don't care if you make three errors and strike out four times today. As long as you play a hundred percent for me and play your ass off, that's all I care about.' That meant a lot to me," Gordon recalled.

Slotted sixth in the lineup and in right field, Gordon preferred left, where he felt more comfortable, but he was grateful to have a spot in right. So how did the return go? Brett Gardner led off the bottom of the first inning and of course hit a ball to right field, down the line for a double. Gordon juggled the ball and Gardner advanced to third. Alex Gordon was charged with an error.

"First ball, leadoff hitter, I was like, '*Are you kidding me*?' I was actually feeling good, and that was my whole goal…not to be a defensive liability," Gordon said, the memory still vivid 10 years later. After the play, he thought, "It can only go up from here." Gordon remembered Yost's belief in him and brushed off the mistake, understanding his long-term goal of being a productive big leaguer.

He hit .222 with seven home runs after his return—nothing special—but Alex gained experience as an outfielder. The birth of his son Max that September made him realize he needed to enjoy the game of baseball more. That perspective and a renewed confidence set the launching pad for his full turnaround in 2011, when he hit .303 with a career-high 23 home runs while earning his first Gold Glove, baseball's prestigious award recognizing the best defensive player at every position. By the time young Max Gordon was two years old, he was crashing into walls at home mimicking the breathtaking catches his dad was making on television on a regular basis at ballparks all around the country.

Max wasn't the only kid trying to be Alex Gordon. Young boys and girls around Kansas City began emulating his every move, wearing his number four jersey and dreaming of one day being the next "Gordo." The same could be said about minor league outfielders throughout the Royals system who were encouraged to watch footage of Gordon. He became the poster child for how to play outfield. No outfielder in the major leagues threw out more baserunners from 2010 to 2020 than Alex. Count his boyhood hero Ken Griffey, Jr. as one of his victims. Gordon lived for silencing the other team's running game and forcing opponents to take a more conservative approach on the base paths. Known for an understated personality, Gordo would make eye contact with a base runner at second base, start to move his right arm in a circle to signal he was warming it up as he silently sent the message, "Keep going, and I'm going to throw you out." He was joking to an extent, but also playing mind games. "I was being serious, and I think they knew it was probably not going to end well," he smiled.

Gordon followed up his Gold Glove in 2011 with repeat accolades in 2012, 2013, 2014, 2017, 2018 and 2019, plus three All-Star Game selections and one of the biggest hits in franchise history. Down 4-3 with one out in the bottom of the ninth against the New York Mets on October 27, 2015, Gordon sent a delirious sold-out crowd at Kauffman Stadium into a frenzy. His home run sent game one of the World Series into extra innings and the Royals ultimately won it, setting the course for the whole series.

More important than any specific moment, Alex became the quiet leader of a team that went from doormat to Cinderella story. Willing and comfortable to talk about or address any issue when needed, and always letting his actions speak louder than his words, Gordon built a reputation centered around hard work. His father, Mike, who passed away in 2018, had told Alex from an early age, "If you're not working hard, someone is getting better than you." So, if coaches asked for seven swings in the batting cage, Alex demanded eight. Ten reps requested by the strength and conditioning coach really meant 11 by Alex's count. An early riser as an adult, Gordon spent his mornings with Jamie, Max, and later, son Sam and daughter Joey. Then, it was all business at the ballpark after lunch. Lifting weights, stretching, hitting in the cage, early defensive work, batting practice where he chased balls in the outfield at game speed like no one in baseball. He then hit, returned to the locker room to relax for 15-20 minutes, hot tub, cold tub, relaxed, stretched again, more cage work and then game time. Every day, over and over, like clockwork. The

media liked Alex but knew tracking him down for an interview could be an impossible task because the timing had to fit his regiment. Teammates also knew not to mess up the routine. So did Jamie.

Gordon played every position in his career except catcher and second base. He even pitched in a pair of lopsided games. But he never returned to third, and never desired a homecoming to that old turf. "Too many evil demons over there that I didn't want to be a part of," Gordon confessed. Actually, he wishes the Royals would have converted him from the beginning, but figures the struggles leading him to the outfield built character and made him appreciate the game even more.

Reflecting back on his career, Gordon said he never questioned himself, but that inner voice of doubt existed just like it does for most people. It occasionally spoke to him during his demotion. *"Is this it for me? Is this not going to work? Should I go back to school, do*

I need to finish my degree....you start thinking about those things because you're put in that life-altering situation, and I was just raised by my mom and dad to put in the hard work."

Gordon announced his retirement September 24, 2020, with four days left in the season. The once-struggling third baseman set to ride off into the sunset as the greatest left fielder of his generation, not to mention the hardest worker. Ned Yost, not one to speak in superlatives, told me, "I've never met a person that was that disciplined that gave that effort every single day no matter what the circumstances were, and I mean never. There was not one time that I can sit here and honestly, quietly say to myself that Alex took a day off. It's unprecedented."

I reached out to 14 former teammates and coaches for comment via text, phone call and Zoom when Gordon made his decision to hang it up officially. Every single one responded, all with heartfelt thoughts. Mike Moustakas, the one-time third-base prospect whose emergence coincided with Gordon's move to left field said, "He taught me about life and how to be a great father and role model. He always did things the right way."

An emotional phone conversation with Alex's mom, an amazing woman and cancer survivor, lasted 30 minutes and included tears from both of us on the call. Leslie Gordon spoke of Alex's grace, humility and legacy of playing the game the right way. "One could not be more proud of a child," she told me, speaking of the second of her four sons. She said she felt that way about all her sons—Eric, Al (as all family members call Alex), Brett, and Derek.

Gordon took the field for the final time September 27, 2020, for his 1,753rd game. Manager Mike Matheny pulled him to start the second inning, allowing Alex to trot off the field to an ovation. Not like the one he received 13 years earlier in his big-league debut. The baseball season of Covid-19 meant Gordon exited the field with no fans in attendance. But the Royals received permission to allow a special group to attend the game. The Gordon family took over a section just as they had back in the old days during those trips in from Lincoln. This time, the nosebleed seats were traded out for multiple suites above home plate. Leslie gushed with pride, tears flowing. Eric Gordon, the oldest of the Gordon boys who held up two fingers to signal Kansas City Royals back on draft day 2005, watched too. Brett, the brother named after George Brett, drove in for the weekend with his wife and kids from Louisiana. Derek, the youngest of the siblings, observed that his advantage over Alex on the links may soon disappear, with big brother expected to transfer his trademark work ethic and discipline to his struggling golf game. George Brett, the Hall of Famer, sat a floor below in a suite with Rusty Kuntz, the teacher. Mike Sweeney watched on television like so many others. Sweeney, the veteran in the Royals clubhouse when Gordon made his big-league debut, summed up Gordon's transformation from third base to left field. "The kid who showed up as the next George Brett became the first Alex Gordon."

Five weeks after playing his last game, Gordon received more news. He would receive a final Gold Glove, tying legendary Royals second baseman Frank White with the most in franchise history. White and Brett are the only two former Royals with statues and their numbers retired. So, where does Gordon fit in team history? I covered "Gordo" for 13 of his 14 years in the major leagues and spent more time with him than any athlete in my career. I'm proud of him as a player and person. Former Royals outfielder Jarrod Dyson echoed my feelings about Alex with a simple statement. "He deserves a statue in KC."

7TH-INNING STRETCH

Time for a quick break from the action to honor the baseball tradition of the seventh-inning stretch. While I promise not to sing "Take Me Out to the Ballgame," which I once nervously butchered as the guest singer at Kauffman Stadium, I *do* want to share a quick story about the importance of gratitude.

I was asked to meet a woman outside the Royals clubhouse in 2012 and was told that she watched me every night on television, but did not speak English. It added up quickly when I learned it was the mother of Royals catcher Salvador Perez. I conversed with Yilda through a translator as she talked about watching me from home in Venezuela, seeing her son routinely dump celebratory Gatorade buckets on players while I interviewed them on the field following a win—a tradition that had become known in Kansas City as the Salvy Splash.

Years later, in 2018, I was gathering player sound bites for Mother's Day, as we always run a feature to honor the moms on our pregame show each season. Days in advance, I approached Salvy in the visiting clubhouse at Camden Yards in Baltimore, asking for a comment on his mom. With a devilish grin to let me know he was messing with me, he said, "It's Tuesday. Mother's Day isn't until Sunday."

I quickly retorted back, "Salvy, as hard as this may be to believe, we actually plan our shows ahead of time and put work into this. I just need 30 seconds."

Not missing a beat, Salvy fired back, "My mom is worth more than 30 seconds, Joel!"

I smiled and agreed, saying he could have all the time he wanted. He suggested that he would have Sunday off from his regular catching duties and could come on with us to do a live interview before the game. My answer was, "Are YOU inviting yourself on to MY show?" All sarcastic and of course, I said "yes."

As Salvy sat down in between Jeff Montgomery and me outside the visitor's dugout on the first base side of Progressive Field in Cleveland, the superstar catcher flashed his usual radiant smile and brought his endless energy. I'd met Salvy as a 20-year-old minor league prospect at spring training back in 2011. He had made one request in his broken English before our interview: "Easy question, sir. Easy question," as I assured him that I would help him out. Salvy quickly became a star on the field when he debuted in the majors in May of that season. He gravitated toward the camera and any moment that might allow him to share his love of life with others. This playful side and huge personality made him an instant fan favorite. But on this Mother's Day, the smiles were only authentic on Perez. Montgomery—a.k.a. Monty—had suffered food poisoning all night at the hotel and was eyeballing a trash can during the interview (too much information, I know, but we've all been there). I was dealing with drama at home and without getting into too much detail, my family was having a real rough morning that made my wife's Mother's Day miserable. So…I was attempting to talk, text, and help in every free moment, even during the commercial breaks of our show. My mind was at home and it was a rare occurrence where I did not want to be at the ballpark. The interview went great and we "faked" our way through it with neither Salvy nor the audience picking up on Monty's sickness or my heartache.

Hours later, when we landed on the team charter back in Kansas City, I grabbed my suitcase and quickly headed to my pickup truck, wanting nothing but to race to the house to see Susan and the kids. As I was about to unlock the doors, I heard a voice and an accent that could only be Salvador Perez's. "Joel, Joel, come here." I walked back over, wondering what he wanted. "Joel, my mom wanted me to tell you thank you for the Mother's Day shoutout and the interview today." It gave me chills. Such a tough afternoon, but I was still able to make an impact on someone else, even through a different language. It was the highlight of my day, and Salvy expressing his gratitude put me in a much better place as I left the airport.

Yilda and I became friends over the years and we frequently exchange messages of well wishes and updates on family, with me looking up Spanish through a translation app on my cell phone so we can communicate. Gratitude will always win the day and is powerful in every language.

Now, back to the action.

BOTTOM OF THE 7TH

Lindsey Roy is an energetic, successful businesswoman who's worked at Hallmark Cards for over 20 years, most recently serving as Chief Marketing Officer. She's down-to-earth, quick to smile, and…bonus for me…a long-time lover of baseball!

Lindsey exemplifies the Small Ball secret and the saying, *When life throws you a curveball, hit it out of the park.* Learn to experience unexpected challenges and difficulties not as dead ends, but as opportunities to evolve. Whether it's in our work or personal lives, when a tough situation arises, we always have a choice: Complain about the disruption, resist change and forfeit the chance to learn and grow from it…*or,* face it head-on, do the hard work of adjusting our perspective, and allow it to transform us in ways we never thought possible.

Lindsey faced a massive curve ball in the summer of 2013 when her life as a successful executive, loving wife and mother of two was painfully disrupted by a traumatic accident—one that would have kept many people in a dark place for a long time. But Lindsey's determination and self-motivation (along with incredible support from family, friends and her Hallmark coworkers) gave her story a positive plot twist that she continues to live out today.

She recalls that life-changing day: "I was on vacation here in the Midwest on the lake…down for a weekend with friends. A series of freak events happened that you just couldn't have predicted, where I was accidentally run over by a boat while I was in the water. My most eloquent way to say that is for a few seconds, I danced with the propeller."

While Lindsey's life was spared, she was left with an amputated left leg, a right leg with about 30% mobility, and a severely injured right arm. She spent two weeks in the hospital, followed by a year of hardcore recovery at home. Fitted for a prosthesis after six weeks, Lindsey started off in a wheelchair as she gradually learned to use the prosthesis, building up to hours of physical therapy. Daily exercises with both a walker and crutches helped her to master a new kind of mobility. Plus, there was work on her severely injured but not amputated right leg, which she describes this way, "I always said it looks like a shark took a bite out of my outer calf." Between skin grafts, tendon transfer surgery and physical therapy that included countless hours of stationary bike riding, stair climbing, leg lift and resistance band exercises, occupational therapy and learning to drive, Lindsey's recovery became a lesson in determination. Add in injuries to her arm, wrist and thumb, and she needed to learn to write with her right hand again. Adaptation became key to her as she considered things like, "*Where do I store my leg when I go to sleep? How do I clean it? What's the best way to shower?*"

How has she adapted? Since her accident, she's zip-lined, snowskiied, snorkeled, and she rides her bike regularly. "I do tend to have a sense of generally what I can do and what I can't as a starting point," said Lindsey.

How did she get to where she is today? How did she hit the curve, and why was it so important to her? "Because the stakes were so high, I clawed myself out of that place by finding different coping mechanisms." She would ask herself questions like, *"How do I get a broader point of view?" "What are ways it could be worse?"* and *"What are things I'm grateful for"*? Lindsey believes strongly in the power of gratitude, especially in life's most difficult moments: "Having that active gratitude mindset and perspective...we talk about it a lot today, but I'm telling you when you're in a hole, it's essential."

She also discovered that we all have a choice: Give up and surrender to the fact that we suddenly have limitations, *or* assess the new situation, be resourceful and make things happen in our own way, however we are able. "You can sit around and say, 'Well, maybe *someday* I will be able to get up and put my kids to bed...'" (Her kids were four and two at the time.) Or, as she learned, you can do what you can with whatever you have. Don't accept defeat; don't see yourself as helpless; make the decision now that whatever life throws at you, you'll find a way through.

"You really don't know how strong you are until you have to be," she says, recalling the discouragement that we all face in our darkest times: "There's absolutely a dip in between Point A and Point B, where you're thrown in the deep end of the pool and you're not ready for it. You're going to struggle...and I struggled."

She believes that storytelling is a powerful way to help each other through. "I think that's part of why we all have to tell each other our stories, because if I can throw you a life raft from something I learned…that makes it all worth it."

Regardless of the traumatic nature of her accident, you won't hear Lindsey comparing her challenges with others. She says that what she's been through has helped her to understand even more that we are all human, all have our own needs, desires and life stories. "I often jokingly say you never meet anyone 90 years old and have them say, 'Gosh, nothing happened in my life,'" she laughs. Facing those dark days not only helped to make her a more compassionate human, but a more understanding leader and coworker.

Though others would describe her as an authentic person even before her life-changing experience, Lindsey says she learned to be even more vulnerable, especially at work. She spoke about her pre-accident life at Hallmark, remembering how she shared only what she felt she should as a leader: "I did this blog that was boring, and didn't put myself out there," she recalls. Very few people took the time to read it. But when she returned with the wisdom and perspective she'd gained from her experience, she wrote from a very real and honest place, "…and everybody read it!" she recalls with a smile. She recognized that, first and foremost, people want to be able to relate to one another as humans, which always includes the good, the bad and the ugly. That's what makes storytelling so powerful. "It's really not useful if people can't put themselves in your shoes," she concludes.

Shortly after arriving home from the hospital, Lindsey was already planning to give a Ted Talk about her experience. Four years later, she walked on stage and did exactly that. Inspiring thousands of people may not have been her original plan in life, but she took what was thrown at her and allowed it to become something that makes a difference in the world. When Lindsey shares her experience, people are deeply inspired, and often line up to tell her about how she has helped them to see their own struggles in a new light. "No matter what accolades anybody gets in life…there's nothing better," she says.

When you hear Lindsey speak, you realize she hasn't just survived, she's learned to thrive: "I think you really do learn to look for that edge; I call it a hidden advantage. Sometimes, it's finding that little strength you have that other people don't, that you can offer the world."

She knows that it's not about what our circumstances are, but how we're looking at them. If there's something that looks 95% bad, we can always focus on that other 5% and make the very best of it.

One year after her accident, Lindsey sat on a beach in San Diego with her family, celebrating their first anniversary of making it through together. Beside her sat a waterproof foot that she uses to protect her prosthetic leg from getting wet. She thought of all the proverbial beach pictures that people post with their feet in the sand, and it gave her an idea. She snapped a pic of her extra foot and penned this caption to go with it:

Live the life you've imagined, even if the details are a little different.

Such a symbolic quote to sum up the journey of someone who not only hit that curve with grace and determination, but uses it every day to help make life more meaningful for those around her.

8 READ THE ROOM

TOP OF THE 8TH

John Hall travels the world as a keynote speaker, and for good reason. He's the co-founder of a time management app called Calendar, co-founder of a content marketing agency named Influencer and Co., and author of the best-selling book, *Top of Mind*. I want to be John when I grow up. (Side note: He's much younger than me.) We were introduced during the Covid-19 pandemic through a mutual acquaintance. I was sitting on my back patio, convincing myself that I was pushing through life without baseball and a paycheck just fine...and then I talked to John. He didn't mean to overwhelm me; actually, he was inspiring and impressive. But when our call ended, I found myself feeling completely unsure about my progress as a speaker. I thought, "Nice guy, but I'm sure I will never hear from him again." A day later he called back wanting to help me. That, in itself, was unexpected, and so generous and uplifting to me—but it was the lessons I learned after that follow-up call that will stick with me forever. John reminded me of so much of the foundation that helped me achieve my television dreams.

He told me when he is giving advice about business and networking, he stresses the importance of understanding what's valuable to people when he calls them, and that oftentimes their answer depends on the day. "Sometimes people don't want to be sold on a Tuesday when you're talking to them, but you want to sell them...They might have just had a really crappy budget week, or they got yelled at by their boss, and then you're trying to sell them." He calls it "value journalism." He went on to explain that a value journalist is someone who tries to figure out what a person values and offers it to them: "If it's sales, sell the crap out of them. Go for it. It's going to be a great sale. If it's not sales and you're being a good journalist, then you better not sell them on that day."

John used to write down the name of every person he met in a spreadsheet, including their story and what they valued. He would test himself on the contents of the spreadsheet and talk about each person's story in his mind so he could remember the details. This activity is now muscle memory for Hall, and these days he spends a few minutes after an initial call with a person to reflect on the conversation before moving on to the next meeting. How guilty am I of ending one meeting and starting the next without a pause? From one Zoom to the next. Or from a coffee to a phone call in the car to the next coffee without ever processing.

John gave me an example. He said that following our initial meeting in April of 2020, he might have thought, "Joel works with the Royals and is excited for baseball to return," and then he would add a calendar notification to text me on opening day to wish me luck. He also said that since he revealed that secret, he probably wouldn't text me! So, I flipped the script. When Major League Baseball returned July 24 during the pandemic, I texted John to tell him opening day had finally come and I wanted to beat him to the punch. I had left a notification in my calendar months prior. I knew he would get a laugh out of it. John continued to help me throughout that summer, and I will forever use his strategy of processing the new connections I make.

It actually occurred to me that I started doing the same thing decades ago. My story involves a three-ring binder and a lot of mileage on an old Honda Civic. I had recently graduated from the University of Wisconsin with one goal, and one goal only: To find a job on television as a sports reporter. There were no TV websites or YouTube links to send resume clips then, or an online LinkedIn community to use for research or messaging. (Yes, I'm old.) So, I used some subscription phone service that posted jobs daily. I applied and mailed resume tapes everywhere...and I received rejection letter after rejection letter. My "aha" moment—or my "put up or shut up" moment—was opening a letter from a television station in Missoula, Montana that once again stomped on my dreams. Nothing against Missoula, but as I sat in my parents' house in Chicago, I thought, "If I can't get a job in Missoula, I'm never going to work in TV." I was heartbroken and thought I might just go manage the local hot dog stand where I'd worked through high school and college...but I made one final attempt and changed my approach.

I started calling small-market TV stations, telling each news director that I was passing through their town soon and asking if they could meet. ("I just happen to be driving through Terre Haute on Thursday...") I really wasn't making that trip until they said, "Sure, I can meet with you." I'm not comfortable cold calling, but my childhood dream was on the line. I visited about 25 stations across the country and must have met 100 reporters, photographers, executives, salespeople and more along the way. I need to confess here that I struggle to remember details in general. To this day, we might be driving around town and my wife will say, "We looked at that house." I usually have zero recollection because we house-hunted 12 years ago. Reality is, I didn't remember those houses 12 *days* later. So, when I need to recall tidbits, I write them down.

That's what I did in 1994. When I walked out of each station, I pulled out this binder I traveled with and jotted down the station name, affiliate, and city, along with every person I met inside... from the receptionist to the news director. It might read:

WJFW, NBC, Rhinelander, WI.

Martin—sports director from St. Louis.

Lance—weekend sports anchor went to Wisconsin.

Heather—weather, real friendly, close to me in age.

Al—news director from Milwaukee who loves sports.

(Al was Al Quartemont, who hired me three months after I wrote that entry in my binder—my first boss at Newswatch 12 in Rhinelander.)

I did this over and over and over. And I added other things to the sheet, like when I sent a thank-you note, the date I made follow-up calls, and details of those conversations. It was like an old-school CRM. To this day, I can still picture faces and people I met a lifetime ago in places like Columbia, Missouri; Binghamton, New York; Rochester, Minnesota; and Quincy, Illinois.

Remembering people truly is a skill that takes a lot of work for me. But it's not enough to remember who they are and what they do. You have to know what they want. As John Hall pointed out, you have to be a value journalist. I call it reading the room.

I have a mantra I live by in baseball that is simply this: *When I walk into the Royals clubhouse, I don't want players walking the other way.* I need to work with these athletes 6-7 days a week for six months straight, at home and on the road. It's a long season, and strategy is key to making sure I don't wear them out. They've never suggested this and no one keeps score, but I just believe this philosophy allows me to be most effective. My sale is the interview and they may not want to be sold to on a given day.

It's not enough to know each player's personality. What's their mood like in the moment? Maybe they have a sick child at home, or a personal issue that's plaguing them. Perhaps it's struggles on the field.

One day my producer told me he needed me to interview Royals third baseman Mike Moustakas about his recent success at the plate. We just needed a short sound bite from Moose. (No one called Moustakas by his first name.) It would only take a minute. When I walked into the home locker room at Kauffman Stadium, I could see based on his demeanor that he was preoccupied or distracted. Not my business to know why, but I made the immediate decision to acquire the interview clip about Moose from the hitting coach instead of Moose himself. (If my pregame-show producer Casey Carter is reading this, I apologize...I sort of never even asked Moose.) But this is a long-game, marathon-type strategy. I felt validated when two minutes after I made my decision to bypass Moose, a local television reporter walked up and said, "Hey, Moose, got a second?" And before he could finish his sentence, I said in my head, "No chance." Moose hopped out of his seat, politely said, "Nope, can't today," and scurried off with a bat in his hand toward the batting cage. A week later in Minneapolis, I again needed something from Moose. As he walked out to the dugout before batting practice at Target Field, he looked as relaxed and upbeat as a player could be. "Hey Moose, you got a second?" Without hesitation, he said, "Yes."

Be a value journalist and read the room. Or, as former Major League Baseball player Raúl Ibañez said to me, "Reading the room is about *feel*. It's understanding when and where, having the empathy piece to know that guy doesn't want to talk today…and knowing the different personalities. If you're a bull in a china shop, you never notice."

BOTTOM OF THE 8TH

A baseball clubhouse provides so many lessons about people and life because of the unique backgrounds found among the athletes.

Raúl Ibañez says it this way: "I think one of the most beautiful things about baseball is some kid from Biloxi, Mississippi winds up having to share a locker with a kid that grew up in San Pedro de Macoris in the Dominican Republic, and now they have a common goal…I think a baseball locker room is the most beautiful setting and the most beautiful place on the planet."

Any given clubhouse can feature men from the United States, Venezuela, Cuba, the Dominican Republic, Japan, Korea, Mexico, and other countries around the world. Cliques based on language, culture or even baseball position (pitchers and hitters get along, but don't always mingle) inevitably occur. Rare is the leader who can unite a diverse group. Ibañez says that such a person has an "ability to connect with everybody and treat everybody the same with courtesy, with dignity, with respect, with empathy. I think it's probably the best thing we can do for our kids is teach them that skill."

Ibañez possessed the very skill he described. Never the loudest man in the room, Raúl had this way of connecting with everyone. From superstar teammates like Ken Griffey, Jr., Albert Pujols and Alex Rodriguez to the bench players. From English speakers to those only fluent in Spanish. Big markets on the coasts to small markets in the middle of America. Teammates, coaches, media and fans have always loved Ibañez as a person. He gives everyone the time of day.

"My parents taught me that. Just, treat everybody the right way. Being able to understand that you have this opportunity to wear a major league uniform and just by saying hello to somebody, or just by talking to somebody, or just by asking them how their day is going…it makes a huge impact. If you have that opportunity, why in the world wouldn't you try to make an impact in somebody's life on a daily basis?"

Raúl and his brothers learned all of life's lessons from their parents as the family ultimately settled in Miami, Florida. "The real gift was the passion and the love and the tireless work ethic," Ibañez said.

Juan Ibañez worked as a chemist in Cuba in the late 1960s before making a great sacrifice for his family's future. Back then, Cubans could leave the country if they worked for their departure, so Juan put aside his primary career and spent two years cutting sugar cane to earn a path to the United States.

Juan and his wife, Moraima, an accountant, moved from Cuba to New York in 1972 with their two sons. "Straight to the boogie-down Bronx," Raul laughed, sharing his family's history. Moraima was pregnant with a third boy during the life-altering trip and gave birth to Raúl on June 2. Forty years later, Raúl would hit a ninth-inning, game-tying, pinch-hit home run for the Yankees in a playoff game not far from where he came into the world.

Both highly educated, Moraima encouraged her husband to return to school in the United States to learn English. He could be a professor or hold any number of jobs. Juan instead found a job sanding furniture within a week of their arrival. "My dad looked my mom in the eye and said, 'I didn't come here to be a burden. I came here to produce.' And that's the cloth I was cut from," Raul said matter-of-factly. The message was simple and powerful. "That was kind of the mantra in our home...go produce, go work, work your ass off, and you can get anything you want in this country."

Juan Ibañez passed away March 24, 1992. Seattle drafted Raúl less than six weeks later in the 36th round out of Miami-Dade College. He signed for $15,000, hoping he could stop the tears his mom shed every day as she mourned her late husband. The son of Juan and Moraima thought, *"I'm going to go for it."* Like his dad, he expected to produce. Raúl remembers being discouraged about his chances from day one in the minor leagues by a speaker at camp. "He said, 'I want you guys to look around.' And there were 40 guys there. 'One, maybe two of you will make it to the big leagues.' And I remember looking around and my immediate thought was, *'Me and who else?'*"

 Raúl made his big-league debut in 1996 for the Seattle Mariners before embarking on a 19-year career that took him from Seattle to Kansas City, back to Seattle, to Philadelphia, on to the New York Yankees, back a third time to Seattle, Los Angeles with the Angels, and one final stint with KC. A player switching teams frequently in baseball means one of two things: He wears out his welcome in a clubhouse, or he is so beloved that management wants him back. Ibañez fit in the second category, a valuable asset to every organization he called home. He also produced on the field as a left-handed bat, averaging more than 20 home runs a season during one 12-year stretch. Raúl hit an impressive 29 home runs in 2013, but after posting a .157 batting average and three homers for the Angels in 2014, L.A. released the veteran a few weeks after his 42nd birthday. His career appeared to be ending until KC came calling again and signed him on June 30, 2014.

Sitting with Raúl at Target Field in Minneapolis and preparing for a live pregame show interview upon his return to the Royals, we laughed at some old footage of his previous stint with the team when

he was in his late twenties and early thirties. Now some of his new teammates were practically young enough to be his sons. I may or may not have made a reference to him being just four weeks younger than me. (Translation: You're old like me, Raúl.) We chuckled, and he gave me plenty of grief right back. If someone had told me on this day that Ibañez would make a major impact on the rest of the season, I would ask about his stats. He would hit .188 with a pair of home runs the rest of the year, which would fail to tell the story. (Remember how the numbers don't always have all the answers—in baseball or business?)

This was supposed to be the long-awaited year for the Royals to regain the relevance in baseball that they'd last held in the 1980s. Between 1995 and 2012, the franchise had finished with a losing record in 17 of 18 seasons. Then, they finally broke through with a winning mark in 2013 and expected to make the playoffs in 2014 for the first time since 1985! On July 22, 2014, the struggling Royals arrived at U.S. Cellular Field to face the Chicago White Sox. Losers of four straight games, Kansas City owned a record of 48 wins and 50 losses. Ibañez, a member of the team for less than a month, decided to speak up and he called a players-only meeting.

So...when is the right time to hold a meeting and address a concern, and how does a leader assure he or she will be heard?

"You can't trick the room," Ibanez responded to my question. "The room will figure you out. That's why I think it's really important to be authentic and to spend time getting to know people, listening to them and observing before you make any changes."

The crux of Ibañez's message focused on this young Royals team not understanding the high level of talent it possessed. "These guys were all winners. It was just getting them together and having a collective vision, and they did all the work," Ibañez told me.

Many years later, I asked Raúl more about his speech on that July afternoon. "The message and the theme of the meeting was, 'If you could see yourselves from the opposing dugout the way that I've seen you...you would understand how great you are,'" he said while reflecting on the memory. "You guys have an opportunity to do something legendary. You have an opportunity to do something extraordinary. You have an opportunity to do something that's going to have an impact on millions of lives," he told a riveted audience. He challenged them to dig deeper: "What are we going to do today... from today on, our goal should be to be the best team in baseball."

Kansas City won that night. Ibanez chipped in a pair of hits as the designated hitter. As a matter a fact, the victory started a five-game winning streak. They would win another eight straight in August. The Royals posted a record of 41-23 from the day of Ibañez's speech until the end of the regular season—third best in MLB.

Corks exploded and champagne flew across the visiting clubhouse in Chicago on the final Friday night of September 2014. The Royals had clinched their first playoff berth in 29 years and ironically, the team celebrated in the same locker room that Ibañez had given his impactful speech months earlier. He looked like a proud father smiling with a cigar in hand as he answered my questions in a live interview.

The Royals won their first eight playoff games in the fall of 2014, eventually losing to the San Francisco Giants in the seventh game of the World Series, falling just short of a championship. Ibanez didn't even make the playoff roster. Players to this day credit him for their success in winning the American League pennant. In 2015, the Royals won the World Championship with Ibañez in the audience, working for Fox Sports as an analyst.

Five years later, he took a trip down memory lane with me during a phone call. "The joy that I felt…watching that collective thing come together, and just being able to be an observer and be a part of it is just one of the most gratifying things. I'm so thankful for that moment. I'm so thankful for that season. I'm so thankful for that group of guys. The clubhouse is probably the greatest clubhouse I've ever been a part of."

He was a huge part. Raúl Ibañez had the feel, and ability to read the room.

9 DO THE RIGHT THING

TOP OF THE 9TH

Patrick Montgomery is a former member of the 75th Ranger Regiment, an elite special operations force...a.k.a. the U.S. Rangers. After enlisting as a 20-year-old, Patrick began an excruciating form of training that mentally and physically tested him to his limits.

The RASP (Ranger Assessment and Selection Program) is an eight-week course that he described to me in one word: "Brutal!" Patrick said he had injuries "coming out of my ears" after finishing the first four-week phase. To be more specific, he sustained a stress fracture in his hip and developed severe shin splints, while still completing the daily task of running five miles. To this day, Patrick says he thinks about those challenges whenever he's struggling and needs perspective. Through that experience, he learned that the limitations we put on ourselves are often only in our heads. Today, he regularly asks himself if it's actually fear that is holding him back from attempting a task or endeavor.

He calls the military a huge business with millions of employees and says the culture in the Ranger Regiment is a true brotherhood. There, Patrick learned to take care of others and to function as part of a system that needs every element to thrive. "You've got to depend on the guys behind you and in front of you to clear a room properly or set up the linear ambush or L-shaped ambush in a correct method to be successful. If you don't, it's your butt and the guy standing to your left and right."

For these soldiers, mutual support is truly a life-or-death matter, and even the most experienced, highly trained individuals will likely face some tragedy along the way. Patrick was no exception. During his first deployment to Afghanistan, his brother-in-law, Jeremy, was killed in a direct-action raid in Paktika Province. Patrick was tasked with taking Jeremy's remains home to his sister. My heart sinks when I think about this story, yet I remember Patrick's unique perspective: "It's probably one of my greatest honors. I don't think I will ever do anything the rest of this life that is more meaningful." He thinks about Jeremy every day, calling him the closest thing he had to a brother. Understandably, Patrick went down a deep, dark path afterward, suffering from survivor's guilt. But through thousands of hours of soul searching, he came to realize that his brother-in-law would want him to lead a productive life that enabled him to take care of his sister and young nephew, who was just six months old at the time.

Patrick is now the CEO of KC Cattle Company, a veteran-owned and -operated organization he founded in Weston, Missouri that raises Wagyu beef. He thinks of Jeremy and chooses to honor him every day by trying to be a good person and by always bettering himself instead of self- imploding. He also takes care of the veteran community by only hiring veterans as employees.

What is Small Ball to Patrick Montgomery? "Just doing the right thing for people." He says there will always be those in business who don't have your best interests at heart but, "being able to recognize that and not let yourself be drawn into that game, maintain your

morals and really just continue to do the right thing" is key. At the end of the day, he says it's about honesty, and being able to put yourself in someone else's shoes.

Patrick and Jeremy used to talk about running a business together. He's doing so today successfully, in Jeremy's honor.

Someone else who has recently inspired me to do the right thing, no matter what the cost, is Kathy Nelson. As president and CEO of the Kansas City Sports Commission, Kathy had to make the unimaginable decision to pull the plug on the Big 12 Men's and Women's Basketball Tournament in March 2020, just as the pandemic hit. She recalls the heavy feeling that day, having to cancel what she called "the Super Bowl of economics every year through sports in our city." Here she was, with these larger-than-life college basketball players looking her in the eye: "I laugh," she said, "they're all a couple feet taller than I am. But they're all hanging their heads, and to see them come out of the locker room to go get back on their buses was just devastating."

Then there were the fans, arriving from across the country to witness an event that generated $20 million of economic impact, just in a small radius of downtown Kansas City. She recalls, "I knew that our board of directors as a non-profit would support the decision, so I wasn't really worried about losing my job, I was worried about other people losing theirs when that's the biggest week of the year for so many financially. I kept going back and forth with... *What's going to happen to the servers at Johnny's Tavern? Or the hoteliers? And how are we ever going to make this up?*" But for Kathy, it came down to the fact that if one person was sick, nothing else mattered. "That's where we had to really focus our attention," she added.

So, in the interest of saving lives, she made the difficult decision to cancel: "Our pastor at church says this often, 'The worst thing is never the last thing.' I had to tell myself that week...*As bad as this feels, this is not the last thing, and it's going to become very small...*but it was hard to think of it like that at the time." She sums it up with her belief that leadership needs to focus on making the right decision and trust that no matter what happens, things will work out.

In hindsight, if they had played that tournament just to appease fans and help the economy, Kansas City may have experienced its Mardi Gras moment with thousands of people packing into an arena, and then returning home to Oklahoma, Texas, West Virginia, Iowa—all the places with schools competing. For Kathy, nothing was worth putting so many lives at risk.

That was one of the great "do what's right" moments I've witnessed, as so many have come to the forefront during Covid-19.

Andrew Dowis is the CEO of Pro Athlete, an e-commerce company that's one of the largest sellers of baseball bats and gloves in the country. They also have one of the best business cultures in Kansas

City. Their massive complex includes a pool, workout room, library, private chef and a bar. It's a simple formula: Take care of your people and give them the freedom to work and play, and trust that they will enjoy the perks without taking advantage of the system. There's always a massive waiting list to work at Pro Athlete.

As the pandemic hit in March, all of its 60 employees were sent home except those in the warehouse who worked socially distanced. Although sales were down 95 percent, the company utilized the Payroll Protection Plan (PPP) to provide relief for two months, ensuring that everyone was paid in full for that stretch. With no baseball being played, athletes around the country didn't need bats and gloves. So, Pro Athlete decided to keep its non-warehouse employees working from home for the rest of 2020. When the PPP money ran out, there were 10 employees who could no longer fulfill their responsibilities from home, and the company considered letting them go. But because the thought of firing employees didn't sit well with management, this company that has always prided itself on "being in it together" offered to pay the employees to stay home and work on several charities in the community. Working on projects like hygiene kits and meals, they were still able to make a difference while avoiding the risk of being in public. So, in essence, Pro Athlete paid employees to perform charitable acts for the community instead of letting them go.

"There was a split second where I might have lost sight of our core values...we had always been built to give back. It was good for morale. The easy thing to do was let them go because we weren't doing anything," said Dowis. Even though Pro Athlete was struggling and suffering as a company, they refused to change who they were. They doubled down to help their own and others. In the end, he said, they'll be known best for doing what matters most: helping people. "[That's] what we will be remembered for, not bats."

Or as my friend Michael Tracy, managing principal of OMNI Human Resource Management, told me early on in the pandemic, "It's a time to build mental equity. How you treat people now will build or take away mental equity later."

Translation: Doing what's right (or wrong) will be remembered more than the score of any game or the closing of any deal.

Patrick Montgomery, the Army Ranger who lost his brother-in-law in Afghanistan, experienced the ultimate blessing during the difficult year of Covid-19. His wife gave birth to the couple's second son in April. Meanwhile, their nephew, Everett, is now nine years old and asks questions about the father he never knew. His mom and grandparents can fill in details about a good man. His Uncle Patrick takes him deer hunting and shares stories of sacrifice and honor. "It's my job to tell him what a warrior his dad was." Everett and his Montgomery cousins will grow up understanding the importance of doing what's right.

BOTTOM OF THE 9TH

Baseball fans won't know the name Monica Ramirez, but Monica is one of the kindest and most impactful people I have met in the sport. I believe she is a saint. Monica never intended to work in baseball. Born in Boston, her parents decided to go back to their home country of Colombia to raise a family when she was four years old. She wanted to be an educator as a young girl and would go on to earn her degree before moving back to the United States in 2001, where she began teaching English as a second language in Phoenix.

She eventually took on work helping young minor league baseball players from Latin America learn English, and that role has evolved over the years into working with hundreds of Kansas City Royals minor leaguers. Back in 2007, well before she would be given major resources and ample space to host classes at the Royals spring training facility, Monica used to teach three sessions three nights a week in a rundown motel with no air conditioning in the sweltering heat of Arizona.

A mother to three boys, Monica could really list hundreds of others she's become a second mom to over the years through her guidance on culture and life skills—not to mention the occasional home-cooked Latin American meal.

Monica remembers those early years, the room usually full of 20 boys, often acting unruly and disruptive. She understood. Being jammed in a tight, hot space didn't help, and these kids just wanted to play baseball. A future World Series MVP, All-Star and Gold Glove catcher named Salvador Perez was among them, as well as an aspiring pitcher named Carlos Fortuna. She held a beginner, intermediate and advanced English class. Fortuna belonged in the advanced, but would stay for all three sessions per night, often spoiling answers for the beginners out of his exuberance to learn English. The students always called Monica "Teacher," "Profesora," "Profi" or "Maestra." Never by her first name, which would be disrespectful in the Latin American culture. When the guys were acting up, Fortuna would always feel terrible and at the end of the night, he would walk up to Monica and say, "Teacher, I'm sorry."

Enter one of my all-time favorite personalities in any professional sports locker room: Bruce Chen. A crafty left-handed pitcher with a huge heart and an endless supply of one-liners (the Royals even ran a "Bruce Chen's Joke of the Day" segment on the scoreboard one season), Chen joined the Royals organization in 2009 with no guarantee of making the big-league team. He broke into the majors

with Atlanta as a 21-year-old in 1998, and played for the Braves, Phillies, Mets, Expos, Reds, Astros, Red Sox, Orioles and Rangers before undergoing elbow surgery and missing his 2008 season. Kansas City gave the 31-year-old an opportunity in 2009, but with no guaranteed contract, Chen was sent to the minor leagues. He never needed to take Monica Ramirez's class. Bruce is of Chinese descent, but he was born and raised in Panama, the son of parents who stressed education first and baseball second. Fully bilingual in Spanish and English, Chen served as an older brother and even father figure to prospects 10 years his junior during the time he was building back his arm and reputation as a reliable pitcher.

As the veteran tried to work his way back to The Show, he befriended Fortuna. Thirteen years separated the two pitchers, but Chen immediately gravitated toward the kid. "Everyone liked him a lot. He was always happy and smiling," Chen recalls.

Bruce earned a spot back in the major leagues with KC in June of 2009. He spent much of the next five seasons with the club, while the 19-year-old Fortuna pitched for the Royals rookie ball affiliate in Burlington, North Carolina that initial season. The two would be reunited in the major leagues in 2011.

Fortuna expected to play for the Royals affiliate in Idaho Falls in 2010 but fainted one day and went to find answers at the Mayo Clinic in Arizona. The tests came back with devastating news. Stage IV liver cancer and a prognosis of six months to live. He was just 20 years old with a baby boy back in the Dominican, and he refused to recognize such a cruel death sentence. Fortuna began to research treatments and found CTCA, the Cancer Treatment Centers of America. The Royals culture is one that stresses doing the right thing, and their response to a minor league player who had gone from talented prospect to no future on the mound backed up their reputation. Monica remembers the message from the team: "They said, 'Anything you need,'" and told him to go wherever he wanted, and they promised to back him up with the necessary resources. So, with the financial and emotional support of the Royals, Fortuna began a more holistic treatment at the CTCA facility in Zion, Illinois, outside of Chicago, coming in from the Dominican or Arizona for two to three days at a time. "He was told he was only going to live six months. They got him almost three more years of life," Monica says. "He loved that place."

Fast forward to 2011. Chen and his teammates knew about Fortuna's prognosis. "All the guys were worried about him," Chen says. Fortuna still wanted to play and be a part of the group, so he was invited to join the big leaguers at spring training camp. The Glass family, owners of the Royals, and the front office took care of his flights, medical expenses and more. "I have nothing but good things to say about the Glass family. They could've released him," says Chen. But there was one missing piece: That big-league dream. Opening day that year fell on March 31, Fortuna's 21st birthday, and the Royals received special permission to allow Fortuna to suit up and sit in the bullpen. A cold, dreary day took so much out of Fortuna that he did not show for the second game. Chen and his teammates wanted him at the ballpark and sent a cab to get him. That second game ended in dramatic fashion with the Royals coming back to win on a walk-off home run in the ninth inning. Fortuna celebrated with his teammates and Chen remembers the words of his sick friend. "This is the best game of my life. I wanted to pitch so badly."

The Royals provided Fortuna with a luxury hotel room, although he often stayed at Chen's apartment unless he was really sick and wanted privacy. Chen knew Fortuna didn't want him to see him suffering at night.

In 2013 Monica received a message from Fortuna, who was back at the clinic in Illinois. "Please pray for me. I'm getting my second blood transfusion today." Monica, trusting her instincts, raced to the ballpark in Arizona and told Royals farm director Scott Sharp that they needed to do something. Sharp had been one of the organization's leaders in caring for Fortuna. Monica flew to Chicago and the Royals arranged for Carlos's mom, Milagros, to fly in from the Dominican Republic.

With his mother and Monica by his side, Carlos was told by the doctor in English, "I really think you should consider just going back home and spending the rest of the time that you have left with your family."

Tears rolled down Carlos's face, but he would not allow Monica to translate the message to Milagros, who only spoke Spanish. Weak and in bad shape, he defiantly told the doctor in perfect English: "You don't tell me when I die. God tells me when to die."

Carlos asked the doctor how much time he believed he had left and received the answer of one to two months. Monica, the saint who had treated this young man as her own son, who had picked up his mother at the airport in Chicago, listened sadly. "How do you process that? I'm there. I don't know what to translate. Mom is there looking at the situation. I didn't know what to do. I didn't know what to say." Monica kept thinking about how Carlos had beat the odds three years before, but she just knew. The cancer had spread from the liver to the lungs.

Flights were arranged and Milagros pushed her son through O'Hare Airport with Monica carrying and dragging all of his heavy bags of baseball equipment, while both women cared for him, making sure he was able enough to fly.

Exactly one month after the doctor's bedside conversation, Carlos Fortuna died peacefully at home in the Dominican Republic on the afternoon of March 24, 2014—a week shy of his 23rd birthday. Before he passed, he could no longer speak, but he put his hands together, signaling to his mother to pray for him.

Seven years later, Bruce Chen told me, "He changed the way I look at things." Retired from baseball, Chen is now the vice president of the Carlos Fortuna Foundation. Scott Sharp is a member of its board of directors. Monica Ramirez, still busy as a mom to her own children and countless others, is the executive director of the foundation.

The Carlos Fortuna Foundation was formed in December of 2019, and it promotes and facilitates parenting training to mothers, fathers, and/or caregivers of youngsters who are enrolled in a baseball academy or program. The organization provides help to families of all different socio-economic levels, but sets its priority in low-income families in Latin America.

RAIN DELAY

One of the beauties of baseball is the lack of a clock. The game finds its own rhythm, often dictated by the pace of the pitcher. I think most players and broadcasters prefer the faster-paced games because the action is more crisp. The defenders, often having to stand out in the scorching heat, appreciate the ability to escape the sun and return to the dugout. Plus, as much as we love baseball, a clean, fundamental contest is more appealing to talk about. And, hey...no complaints... but getting back home or to the hotel before midnight sure beats the early morning hours!

Rain can change those plans. One positive of delays for me is the chance to catch up with scouts who are in town to watch the game, or to visit with opposing broadcasters and writers. Sitting around and swapping stories that often go back decades always makes the time more enjoyable...although it's safe to say we ran out of stories on May 30, 2013. In the midst of a losing skid, Kansas City had just replaced their hitting coaches in the afternoon with iconic former third baseman George Brett to serve as the interim coach. Brett drove across the state of Missouri for the series finale against the St. Louis Cardinals. Little did he know his first night on the job would include working multiple early-morning hours. The game started in a one-hour delay and nearly made it to the end. With radar showing a large amount of rain rapidly approaching, St. Louis took the field ahead 2-1 in the ninth inning. Kansas City scored three runs to take a 4-2 lead and before the Cardinals could even record an out, the skies opened and the rain fell...and fell...and fell. Confusion over some rules ensued, but to sum up the basics—a delayed game between two teams that are playing for the final time of the year against each other (which was the case for the Cardinals and Royals) is required to revert back to the last full inning completed. Translation: The Royals' runs would not count, and the Cardinals would be awarded a 2-1 win if the umpires deemed the game unplayable to completion.

Longtime veteran ump Joe West was ready to call the game, but Royals Manager Ned Yost, with a keen ability to read a radar due to his love of hunting, pointed out to West that a break in the rain might occur. West and his crew looked at the field multiple times after midnight and eventually gave the go-ahead to prepare the nearly flooded surface. With more rain closing in, the Cardinals grounds crew appeared to move in slow motion, giving Kansas City the impression they were stalling to let the next storm stop the contest. Somewhere in the 2 a.m. hour, Royals players started carrying bags of dirt to the infield in order to dry the surface and speed up the process. Other players handed out sunflower seeds and gum to the couple dozen fans left in the stadium in a setting suddenly more intimate than a high school baseball game. The Cardinals' perceived lack of interest in finishing the game definitely motivated West to find a way to play. He told me years later, "I wasn't going to let KC lose like that." Play resumed at 3:04 a.m. and from my spot in the camera well next to the third-base dugout, I could hear Cardinals radio announcer Mike Shannon's voice bouncing off the concrete walls of the concourse above, echoing in every direction. A faint chant of "Let's Go, Royals" from the handful of Kansas City fans still standing filled the air. The Royals wrapped up the ninth inning and won 4-2. As the game ended, I sent out a tweet. "And we are done. Royals Live next!!!" The time stamp read 3:14 a.m. West's crew hopped in a limo and slept on the 300-mile drive to Wrigley Field before working an Arizona Diamondbacks-Chicago Cubs *day game*, just 10 hours after walking off the soggy Busch Stadium infield. Prior to first pitch at Wrigley, West told both teams, "There will be no rebellion today," meaning the umpires were tired and would not look fondly on any arguments.

We left the stadium and flew to Dallas, arriving at the team hotel around 8 a.m. I did a live interview for a Kansas City sports radio

station after I arrived in my room, and I nearly fell asleep while on the air. I woke up sometime in the afternoon and made my way to Rangers Ballpark in Arlington for the Royals' 7 p.m. game that evening, still only half awake.

The delays the night before, while not ideal, reminded me about the beauties of baseball. You never know what might happen on any given night. Nothing ever goes quite as planned. Someone is always watching (as my Twitter feed showed after three in the morning!) The Royals broke their eight-game losing streak in the wee hours of that morning and started a string of winning 13 of the next 18 en route to their best season in 10 years.

I promise no more rain delays in this book, but this *will* go extra innings, or as we often say at the stadium when a game goes beyond nine: free baseball.

⑩ DON'T GIVE UP

TOP OF THE 10TH

Ask Carlos Vides where his career as a highly successful salesman began, and he'll paint a vivid picture of an eight-year-old boy in Honduras, barefoot in the street, selling what he could to help provide for his family. "If you've ever been to any third-world country… and you see those kids running around selling stuff…fruits and vegetables…that was me. "

He explains, "My mom and dad, neither one of them knew how to read or write, so all they knew was work." And after a whole day on the street, he might be allowed to keep just five cents, so young Carlos didn't have much to show for those long hours. But he was taught that if you work hard and don't give up, things will take care of themselves. And work hard, he did.

At 13, two big things happened: He got his first pair of shoes from some U.S. missionaries, and he decided to invest in his future by becoming an electrician. He worked a job for a man who had moved to New York City, got a job washing dishes, and returned with enough money to build a big house in Honduras. When he told Carlos how much an electrician could make in the U.S., the boy's interest was piqued.

But obtaining a visa required at least $75, just for an appointment. "You're automatically turned down if you don't have that kind of money," he recalls. Refusing to be discouraged, 15-year-old Carlos found a way.

His plan included raising a pig given to him by his mother, which he sold for 250 pesos and used the money to make his way to the United States. With only a map and a backpack, Carlos and two friends crossed Mexico on foot for three and a half months, finding odd jobs to support themselves along the way. Carlos arrived in the U.S. as a minor—no parents, immigration papers, or ability to speak English.

He sought help from churches, schools and anyone who was willing to lend a hand. He found a job in Alexandria, Virginia, sanding walls to be wallpapered, and used what little money he made to help him learn English…his number one goal. "I bought a little Walkman," he remembers, and tells about listening to ESL tapes on it all day, every day, while he worked. His goal was to learn 100 new English words per day.

His English improved but the $150-$200 a week of income earned sanding walls wasn't cutting it, so at the end of 1990, he met some men who suggested a move to New York, where more opportunity, a larger community and easier transportation options provided hope. With $22 to his name, Vides hopped on a Greyhound bus in January of 1991. It was a cold winter night when he arrived at Grand Central Station all alone, but not scared of the large crowds. "I was in my own zone. All I cared about was get directions and move on," he says. Able to communicate in broken English, he asked around about any Spanish-speaking people and found someone who was willing to give him a place to sleep for the night with the condition that he leave the next day.

First thing in the morning, he bought a newspaper and started reading the "Help Wanted" ads. He laughs, "I had an English teacher that used to tell me, 'When they ask you what you can do for a job, say, "Anything."' A local Dunkin' Donuts was hiring, so Carlos applied, and when the man asked, "What can you do?" he answered, "Anything!" So, for $4.50 an hour and all the coffee and donuts he desired, he was hired to clean the kitchen.

Soon, he was using his limited English and natural people skills to serve customers up front.

He recalls telling the manager, "Teach me anything; I want to learn everything about Dunkin' Donuts." So, he learned how to be a baker and take inventory. He also signed up for nighttime English classes— two hours, three days a week. He mastered customer service and became assistant manager within six months. In about a year, the owner asked him to manage one of his stores. Eventually, Dunkin' Donuts paid for Carlos to go to management school in Boston, and he started running eight different stores, teaching other people everything he'd learned.

In October of 1998, he moved to Kansas City to be near his sister, who'd also come to the U.S. Carlos began working as a baker at Price Chopper, where he met his future wife. The store's policy did not allow co-workers to be in a relationship. So, he applied to be a car salesman at the well-known Cable Dahmer Dealership, was interviewed and hired on the spot. Carlos became the number-one salesman seven years in a row.

Meanwhile, he got married in 1999 to Michele, the woman he'd worked with at the grocery store, who happened to be an American citizen. He applied for papers to live legally in the U.S., but never heard back from the government. The Videses welcomed a baby daughter into the world, bought a house and a car, and paid taxes. Carlos Vides was living the American dream. "Life was just fantastic," he says. In 2011, following the terrorist attacks of September 11 in New York, he received a letter stating that he'd been approved; his family was invited to the immigration office for a green card interview. He was asked to bring proof of marriage, bank accounts and tax records...but they never looked at his documents. Upon arrival, his family quickly discovered the real reason for being summoned. "I never saw it coming," he says, remembering their question:

"You know what you're here for?"

"Yes! For my interview!" he'd responded.

Then, the authorities stated that he was an illegal immigrant, handcuffed him, and put him in jail. "My wife is crying and I'm like, 'It's going to be ok. I'll be back.'" During the dark days that followed, Carlos held onto the hope that he would somehow make it through. He was sent to Leavenworth Prison where, "I became the psychologist, mentoring the guys...how to think when they got out of there, how to write a book or open a business."

Despite his determination to stay positive, when he was finally released from prison and deported to Honduras, it was "the lowest point in my life." Separated from his wife and baby, with no idea how he would make his way back, Carlos refused to give up.

He found work at a Chevy dealership in Honduras where (unlike the U.S.) they sold about one car a month. With his signature mix of positivity and product knowledge, Carlos was soon selling more than anyone. He became a manager. "I started recruiting and training other people, and in a few months, we're selling over 20 cars a month."

Meanwhile, in the United States, his wife was feeling discouraged. They tried everything they could think of. Carlos held onto his belief and told her, "It's gonna happen!"

And then, it did! He told his story to the right person at the right time: "The main priest in Honduras came to buy a car from me and said, 'Son, I never do this, but I know the ambassador.'" A few days later, Carlos was summoned to the embassy, they handed him his passport and said, "Welcome to the United States."

After 14 months, Carlos Vides was reunited with his family in an indescribable moment he says felt like "winning a Super Bowl." He returned to working in sales and rose in the ranks at both Cable Dahmer and New York Life Insurance, where he later became a marketing consultant. No matter where he goes, Carlos is known for his determination, his positive outlook and his signature smile.

Today, Carlos works as a financial advisor and also began a speaking career, putting his energy into inspiring and developing people. "My biggest thing is to grow kids," he smiles. When he recognizes a young person with good work habits and the desire to succeed—even if they don't have much else—he takes them under his wing and teaches them. "It's been the most rewarding part of my life."

He wants people to know that it's not about what you have to begin with, it's about what you make. He encourages them to dream big: "Write down the things you want out of life." And he is adamant about integrity: "Always do the right thing. No matter who you talk to or what you do, if you do it with the right intention…things will come around for you." He says the most important thing he's learned is, "How to be humble, how to appreciate everybody around you, and how to always, always offer help."

He sums it all up very simply: "Everything is possible." If that barefoot, 8-year-old boy from Honduras believed it, we surely can too.

BOTTOM OF THE 10TH

Whit Merrifield entered the latter part of a spring training game for the Kansas City Royals in 2015 as a replacement for star first baseman Eric Hosmer. Drafted in 2010 by the Royals out of the University of South Carolina in the ninth round, Whit turned pro after playing the role of hero in the College World Series. He'd delivered the game-winning hit against UCLA in the 11th inning to give his school its first national baseball championship.

On this day, St. Patrick's Day, 2015 against the Cubs, Whit was still trying to earn a ticket to the big leagues in spring training. He had spent the previous five seasons grinding away in the minor leagues and would soon be sent back again. As he trotted out to play defense, the Cubs first-base coach passed on a message from Chicago's manager Joe Maddon (whose story appears in Chapter 4.) The coach said Joe wanted to know if Whit's father was Bill Merrifield.

Whit's dad had played for Maddon in the minor leagues back in the 1980s as an infielder in the California Angels organization. Drafted by the Pittsburgh Pirates in the 36th round in 1980, Bill Merrifield opted to attend Wake Forest University instead. He dreamed of playing football, but at 6'3", 165 pounds, Bill found a home on the diamond as an infielder with Wake. Back then, the school only gave three baseball scholarships and Bill received half of one. The team featured a bunch of future lawyers, doctors, accountants and more than a dozen football players looking for an activity so they could avoid spring workouts. Wake's tight end doubled as the right fielder. Future NFL punter Harry Newsome played third base. Bill Merrifield eventually earned a full scholarship and All-ACC conference honors twice, and he was selected by the Angels in the second round of the 1983 draft. He hit 29 home runs for Maddon and the Peoria Chiefs in Single-A ball a year later.

Bill advanced to Triple-A baseball, the highest level of the minor leagues, and in 1987 was traded from the Angels affiliate in Edmonton to the Pirates AAA team in Vancouver. After three games, he received the call all minor leaguers dream about during those long bus rides of a season that features small paychecks. (Bill received about $600 per month in the minors.) Pittsburgh summoned him to the major leagues. His wife, Kissie, still in Edmonton, drove across North America to meet her husband as Bill took flights all day from Vancouver to Salt Lake City to Dallas to Atlanta to Pittsburgh. No money in his pocket, he arrived at Three Rivers Stadium on September 1, 1987, having never been to a big-league stadium. He walked into the administrative office to ask for money to pay for his cab and the response was, "Who are you?"

He entered the Pirates' clubhouse and was asked to work out and hit for the coaching staff. Manager Jim Leyland observed. After returning to his locker, Bill met his new teammates—players like Barry Bonds, Andy Van Slyke and Bobby Bonilla. As he took ground balls in the infield, chatting with Bonilla, rain forced a cancellation of the batting practice. "The equipment guy comes up to me and goes 'What do you need? You're starting at first base tonight,' and I was like, 'Oohh, okay,'" Bill recalls. About 45 minutes later, he received another message. "The clubbie comes back to me and goes, 'Skip [Leyland] wants to see you in his office.'" I'm thinking we are going to go over signs, we're going over strategy," Bill recalls. "First thing out of his mouth, he goes 'Bill, we want you to prove you can hit for power.'" Bill figured he would spend the month of September playing for the Pirates, but Leyland wanted him to ship out in a few days to an instructional league to fine-tune his skills. There would be no Major League debut.

In an era without websites and scouting video, Bill now figures the Pirates wanted to get an up-close look at their new acquisition and they didn't like what they saw in the workout. "I turned around and walked out. I walked to my locker, and my sh*t was already packed. It was already in my bag," he recounts, laughing at the 33-year-old memory. Merrifield retreated to the hotel and watched Zane Smith, the Braves pitcher he thought he would face, throw a complete game shutout against the Pirates. When his wife finally arrived after the cross-continent drive, not knowing the news (no cell phones), the young couple hopped back in the car, drove to Florida and rented a fishing shack on the water as Bill joined the instructional league.

A year later, now playing for the Texas Rangers' Triple-A affiliate following a trade, Bill Merrifield broke his foot sliding into second base. With a recovery of five months, the 26-year-old told his wife, "I'm out." He wanted to focus on raising a family.

———

Whit Merrifield called his dad on September 1, 2015, to talk about his own crossroads. That date is 28 years to the day from when Bill nearly cracked the Pirates lineup. Unlike many of his minor league teammates, Whit did not receive a September callup to the Royals in 2015. "That can really dig at you if you let it, and quite frankly, I let it," he says.

The younger Merrifield told his father about the soon-to-be-completed minor league season, "When it's done, I'm not turning around and coming back," as he contemplated moving on from baseball at the age of 26, just like his dad.

Dad replied to son, "I will support you in whatever you want to do, but just make sure that if that's your decision, then make it for the right reason, because you can't go back. Baseball is going to go on whether you're playing or not." The words that stuck with Whit from his father were, "Once you take [your cleats] off, you can't put them back on."

Whit guesses he returned home to North Carolina 50/50 on whether to continue his career, and he chose to push forward. "My dream was to be a professional athlete…I just loved to compete. I loved to be the best. Baseball was what I was best at," he says.

Determined to achieve his goals, Whit dedicated the offseason to adding power to his versatile game by tweaking his swing and following a strict diet consisting of a giant plate of eggs and oatmeal for breakfast daily for five months followed by chicken, rice and vegetables every two to three hours and a large dinner in the evening. "It was grueling. It was horrible," he recalls, but he added 20 pounds of muscle and returned to spring training with added strength and confidence.

In May 2016, Bill and Kissie Merrifield hopped in the car for a long drive, just like they had done following the disappointment in Pittsburgh. This time, a Merrifield would play in the big leagues. Their son had begun the year in Triple-A but finally received the call to The Show. Only problem…Kissie lost her wallet, meaning a flight would be impossible without proper identification. So, the proud parents drove nonstop from their home in North Carolina to Kansas City to watch Whit make his MLB debut in the second game of a doubleheader against the Boston Red Sox. He batted ninth, played left field and recorded his first hit. When the game ended, the Royals immediately flew to Chicago for their next series. The Merrifields jumped back in the car and extended their trip, driving to the Windy City.

Whit was sent back to the Triple-A team in Omaha in July for five weeks and he began 2017 in Nebraska once again, but this time the Royals recalled him to the big-league club in mid-April and he never returned to the minors. He progressed from a role player just trying to earn a spot on the roster, to fighting for playing time, to eventually becoming an irreplaceable leadoff hitter for the Royals. Whit Merrifield posted the most hits of any player in 2018, and not just on the Royals team—the most of *any* player in the majors. For anyone wondering if Whit's year was a fluke, he followed up 2018 by leading MLB again in hits in 2019. Only one other right-handed batter in the game's history led baseball in hits in consecutive seasons. The late Kirby Puckett, a future Hall of Fame outfielder, accomplished the feat from 1987-1989.

Bill and Kissie joined Whit in Cleveland in 2019 when he played in his first All-Star Game. (They flew this time.) They rarely miss a game on TV, which is a lot, because Whit plays every single one, rotating positions but always leading off and always driving opposing pitchers crazy with his consistent ability to hit the ball.

"For me to watch Whit live his dream of being a professional athlete and putting it in people's faces that he was good...and *better* than people said, that was more fun than me ever doing it," Bill reflects.

Whit Merrifield became the leader of the Royals, the star player who always spoke to the media during good and bad times, and a true success story. Had it not worked out, he says he would've found some other kind of job in sports. But he never gave up on his dream to play.

"I'm glad I didn't."

11 EVERY ROLE MATTERS

TOP OF THE 11TH

Mike Matheny sat with the clubhouse staff cleaning off cleats one day after a spring training workout in 2020, his first year as Kansas City Royals manager. His willingness to do the "dirty work" perfectly illustrates the message of a book called *Legacy*, written by James Kerr. Kerr shared powerful lessons in leadership he'd learned after being embedded with one of the world's most successful rugby teams. Matheny, after being named manager of the Royals on October 31, 2019, suggested the book to some of the veteran players he would soon be leading. Kerr wrote in the book, "Sweep the Sheds: Never be too big to do the small things that need to be done." Here was Matheny in Surprise, Arizona, sweeping the sheds, so to speak.

This reminded me of a conversation I had with Jake Reid about Small Ball on my podcast a year earlier. Reid, the president and CEO of the professional soccer team Sporting Kansas City, spoke about the club's owner Cliff Illig. "Cliff says one line that sums it up—'Everybody picks up trash.' That sounds completely bizarre, but what he means by that is this: our venues, we want the experience to be pristine for folks, and I remember vividly seeing him [Illig] walking across the field and bending down to pick up a piece of confetti, which, by the way, we fire after every goal so there's a lot of confetti!"

What Reid witnessed that day was a leader who truly believed that no one is above any task, no matter how seemingly insignificant it may be. Those who set that example will lead organizations of people who do the same, and will create a culture that values every person, regardless of their role, and every task, regardless of its size.

Small Ball secret: *Every role matters from top to bottom.* An effective leader not only understands this truth, but embodies it, no matter who is watching.

During my USO trip to Kuwait in 2018, we were visiting with an Air Force colonel as F-16s took off outside the building. I remember former Royals first baseman Mike Sweeney asking the colonel what those pilots were working on that day. The colonel said, "We don't practice over here; they're going over to bomb targets in Syria." What a sobering realization for us as civilians, catching an inside glimpse of another world.

He then told us that there were 20 pilots on site (including him), a dozen F-16s, and over a thousand service men and women to make it all work. I realized that while everyone might want to be Tom Cruise's character, Maverick, from Top Gun (and that's exactly what this guy looked like!), there were so many other people working in the wings who were just as important, but rarely recognized.

When I ask someone what they do, and they answer, *"I'm just the...,"* I know they are so much more than that, even if they don't realize it. I don't think people give themselves enough credit, especially if it's a low-profile, under-the-radar job.

The chef in the Air Force is not *just* the chef. If he or she doesn't cook a good meal, we don't want to imagine the discomfort those pilots are going to go through up in their fighter jets.

If the engineers and maintenance people don't do their jobs right, and the air conditioning fails in 115-degree heat, then no one sleeps at night, and those pilots won't be alert and at their best. It's the same for the mechanics, the military police, and every single other role. Every one of those jobs has potential life-and-death implications at a base in the Middle East.

After our USO visit, a senior airman sent me a handwritten letter that said, "My squadron takes care of all the maintenance here, and if we don't do our job right, we're living in prehistoric times." And I knew exactly what he was talking about.

Every role matters from top to bottom and everywhere in between. The more we acknowledge this—whether it's in our own work or appreciating someone else's—the more valued people will feel, and the more we will all be inspired to give our best, whatever we are doing in life.

I see this take place in the sports world all the time.

Take Christian Colón, for example. He was a first-round draft pick of the Royals in 2010 out of Cal State Fullerton, a high-character person who fit the type of player the team values. Colón never amounted to the star status of other high selections, yet he epitomized the importance of a role player when it mattered most.

During the 2015 season, Colón batted 119 times (which was about one-quarter of the opportunities of the starters). His final plate appearance of the regular season took place in the last game of the year as the Royals wrapped up their schedule in Minnesota. Colón entered the game as a pinch hitter in the seventh inning and singled. He added a walk in the ninth in what would be his final appearance for weeks.

He returned to the plate 28 days later. This was the Royals' 14th playoff game of the postseason. They had played in 151 innings of nail-biting action, and in their 152nd inning, Colón was called to pinch hit for pitcher Luke Hochevar, a former first-round pick himself. The Royals had won three of the first four games of the World Series against the New York Mets and found themselves tied 2-2 at New York's Citi Field in the 12th inning. With one out and a runner on third, Colón's first and only playoff at-bat resulted in a hit to break the tie, and the Royals added four more runs after Colón's magical moment.

Christian Colón played a lesser role than what was perhaps envisioned back on draft day in 2010. Luke Hochevar became an excellent reliever. Not exactly the job he expected when the Royals drafted him first overall in Major League Baseball in 2006 to be a starting pitcher. But the record books will forever show Colón with the game-winning hit to give the Royals their first World Championship in 30 years. The winning pitcher was Hochevar.

———

I was 22 years old when I landed my first television job as a news reporter at a TV station in Rhinelander, Wisconsin. I won't mention my starting salary, but I will say I figured out quickly that I'd need a roommate, because my $300 apartment rent was too much!

And let me tell you (as a lot of start-up entrepreneurs can attest to!), I was wearing every hat. While I was initially hired as a news reporter and soon a sports reporter, I was also my own cameraman, video editor, anchor…and I wrote all my scripts. Nowadays, we have people running cameras, others editing, engineers that may just focus on lights, and others running audio. It takes so many behind-the-scenes individuals to make a show happen, and fans at home may never know their names. It's easy to take their work for granted when things are running smoothly, but if something sounds wrong or looks "off," we're quickly reminded of the importance of every task.

I often hear from people watching our baseball broadcast who say, "How do you guys find all that information? How do you know so much?" I tell them that our broadcast team wakes up every morning of a game to a seven-page email attachment that contains every stat, match-up, and piece of history we could possibly want. It's created by David Holtzman, our associate producer of baseball information and graphics, someone who truly makes us smarter daily. And if you see interesting numbers on the screen, it's the work of Al Broughton, our graphics wizard.

Watch any sporting event on TV and just spend 30 seconds to a minute counting how many times the shots change, and you'll understand how much work goes into that process. When it's done well, a viewer won't even notice the camera cuts because it is so smooth and seamless. That's the director's role—another unsung hero in this business. He or she is basically managing all the camera operators and all the technicians. While the producer is in charge of content and talent, the director is leading the crew behind the scenes, and that's no easy task.

I've worked with numerous producers during my Royals tenure, most recently Casey Carter, who handles our pre- and postgame shows masterfully and with pure joy and positivity every day, and Kevin Cedergren, our game producer who brings consistency and structure to the broadcast. But the quiet man who really makes us go is Steve Kurtenbach, who has directed almost every game I've been a part of since he re-joined the team in 2009. Steve began directing television in 1983 and baseball in 2003. He has the calmness of a surgeon amidst the chaos that occurs in live TV, where anything can go wrong at any moment. He never panics and his demeanor and experience are two of the reasons that technical crews across the country rave about our group. Fans would not recognize Steve or know his name other than the fact that we mention it at the end of a broadcast…but he is irreplaceable.

Sam Abramson is our EVS operator in the TV truck. In short, he's one of the men and women who create the slo-mo replays and highlight packages during a show. Along with being my row mate on charter planes and the two of us being born just hours apart, Sammy is known as one of the best EVS operators in the country. I joke with him all the time that if a squirrel runs onto the field, he'll have a highlight put together within 30 seconds, flashing back to last time it happened. That may seem like an exaggeration, but those kinds of things happen on a regular basis with Sammy. He possesses this incredible memory of where every highlight is stored, and he can find it in a matter of moments.

Who are the people in your world that fly under the radar like that— who don't want the attention, but are absolutely key to your success? Those are the roles that matter more than we realize, in any walk of life. Organizations win with the Christian Colóns of the world. Or as James Kerr wrote in *Legacy*:

"We might ask ourselves if excellence—true excellence—begins with humility; with a humble willingness to sweep the sheds."

BOTTOM OF THE 11TH

I caught up with Peter Clune a few months into his new role leading Lockton, a family-owned Kansas City company with a rich history that's known for being a phenomenal place to work. The way he described his first days as CEO of the world's largest privately held insurance brokerage firm was so telling about his characteristics as an authentic leader. When asked what kind of message he delivered to his approximately 7,500 employees after his promotion in May of 2020, he answered that it wasn't about giving a speech to them. Rather, it was about him listening to what *they* wanted to say. "In 90 days, I've had about 250 one-on-one meetings…I ask people, 'If you were in charge, what would you do?'" he said, and added, "Instead of trying to be more interesting, I try to be interested." Bottom line: Peter knows how to empower every person in the company, regardless of their role, by showing them that what they contribute personally matters. And not only that…he trusts that they are the ones who know what needs to happen on the front lines because they are much more entrenched in the action. "Corporate doesn't know what our clients need. The people working closest to them do," he said.

He credits founder Jack Lockton for laying that kind of foundation. "Early on, Jack said that we are not going to build a company where the center of the company tells people what to do. It's going to be about empowering people. Let's let *them* make the decisions…Our most important people are the people closest to our clients. That's a big foundation of the culture."

People love working at Lockton because they feel that sense of inclusion and ownership. To play a role there isn't about fitting into a box or following a set of rules, but about being trusted to do what you do best for the good of the team. It's about being able to say, "This is what I have to contribute," and knowing it won't be dismissed but rather heard, and valued. "It's so much more fun when it's about people taking care of each other, winning together," Peter reflected on the mutual support they share. "All the leaders here get up every day trying to protect that."

And as he leads, he openly admits that he doesn't get it right all the time. He owns his imperfections, giving others the courage to own theirs. "No one wants to hear about that perfect person," he said. "Business is a grind. You have to be willing as a leader to say, 'You know what...I screwed up.'" He isn't afraid to try things, and doesn't want his employees to be, either. He encourages them: "We're going to fail, but when we do, just admit it and dust yourself off and move on." That permission gives everyone the breathing room to explore the potential of their role.

Peter also lives the example of respect for every person in the company. He believes that in order to sustain a thriving culture anywhere, we need to give one another the courtesy of our undivided attention. This sends a huge message to others that they are worthy of our time, and that whatever they have to say truly matters to us. He makes it a point to get rid of any potential distractions (even his phone!) when meeting with others, and to be "present at every interaction." Because, he concludes, "Culture is this combination of 10,000 interactions."

And that's the kind of culture he was hired to ensure: "The direction I get from the Lockton family is really simple. Make sure this is an awesome place to work, make sure it's a great place for our clients, and make sure we're giving back to the community nonstop. As the CEO, it's a pretty easy job. I'm just keeping the tradition alive."

In fact, Peter believes that one reason the family chose him to take the reins of their company was his wholehearted belief in Jack Lockton's philosophy of empowerment. He shared the perfect (baseball related!) illustration of how that belief was already forming during his childhood. It involves a trip down memory lane to the 1980s visiting clubhouse at Kauffman (then Royals) Stadium. No one knows what it's like to play a behind-the-scenes role quite like a baseball clubbie, and that's what young Peter experienced as a teen.

His dad, Pete, Jr., was the attendant in the visiting locker room at old Municipal Stadium in Kansas City back in the 1960s. He recalled all that the job entailed, explaining, "Not only do you unpack the teams every three days, you serve them meals. In the '60s this was probably pre-catering, so my grandma would take the same three meals out to the visiting locker room each game. I knew as a kid that if I could get down to my grandpa's house at the first inning, he'd be driving the food out to the game." All those stadium visits piqued his interest, and when his Uncle Tom took over running the visiting clubhouse in the late '70s, Peter convinced him to give him a shot as a clubbie. And he'll be the first to tell you it was not a glamorous job.

Baseball fans see those bat boys and girls during a game and may think all they do is run back and forth, snagging baseballs and picking up equipment. What they *don't* see is the behind-the- scenes work. Here's what it's like to work in a big-league clubhouse: That kid arrives in the afternoon, sometimes coming straight from school like Peter did. They prepare for 81 games in a season and then do tedious jobs late into the night, like knocking the mud off the players' spikes, shining shoes, vacuuming the clubhouse, picking up laundry, running errands for players and doing anything needed to allow the athletes to perform at the highest level. The hours can include middle-of-the-night work to unpack an arriving team's equipment in the wee hours. Clubbies learn to tackle tasks that are often taken for granted and usually go unrecognized (although the tip money sure can be nice for a kid). They do them because that's their job and they are a part of the team, even if it's out of the limelight. Peter learned to roll up his sleeves and do whatever it took to play his part.

He also was taught the value of remembering the "little guy." Clubbies pay less attention to the stats or results, instead focusing on the relationships. Ask anyone who's worked in a baseball locker room about their favorite players and they could talk for days, sharing stories and encounters. Although, keep in mind that much of their material may be kept private…what goes on in the clubhouse, stays in the clubhouse.

The term "bat boy" is a bit silly because most clubhouse "kids" are later high school or college age, but they all take note of how they are treated. Did the player talk to you? Did they remember your name when they came back to town? Peter recalled how visiting team players, dressed in their suits and ready to depart to their next destination, would stop and take a moment to track him down to show their appreciation. "They'd give you 10 or 20 bucks…and say, 'Peter, I just want to say thanks.'" It clearly made an impression on the teenager, because a few decades later, it's obvious that Peter believes in creating and sustaining a level playing field, where everybody matters and knows it.

"I think the leaders of today… that have the most success are not only going to be the ones who are good at their skill sets and understand the technical aspects of their job, but they're going to be the ones who can really connect with people, really inspire people, really bring a locker room type setting, meaning we're all on the same team." He said that he learned a lot of that during those years in the clubhouse, not to mention being able to observe the different leadership styles of managers—which he admits didn't resonate then, but left a long-term impression.

I can't end the story without mentioning the highlight of Peter's baseball career—working the 1985 World Series. Take a look on YouTube for some grainy nostalgia or break out those old VHS tapes, and you'll see him appear as a ball boy on the first-base line. One of his fondest memories of that special time involved an experience with someone who took the time to care for a young, hard-working kid just doing his thing. Peter, being left-handed, was always using a strange glove and unbeknownst to him, Royals pitcher Bud Black (a southpaw himself) had noticed. As they celebrated that World Series victory the night of game seven (working in the visiting clubhouse doesn't exclude a clubbie from ultimately being a part of the Royals organization), Black pulled him aside and handed him a special glove he'd chosen for Pete. "I still have it today," he smiled, "I never forget things like that."

I'm willing to bet that the folks at Lockton don't forget those moments with Peter, either. And it's not about him impressing them with a fancy job title; it's about them feeling valued. It's about someone taking the time to be present with them, listen to their needs and ideas, and acknowledge that what they contribute matters.

Jack Lockton created the company with his family name in 1966. He valued entrepreneurship, hard work and passion with a focus on people. Revenue reached $600,000 by 1976 and $6 million in 1986. By 2020, that number hit $2 billion, making it the only privately owned billion-dollar insurance broker in the world. The Lockton commitment from day one and years after Jack's passing is "to provide the most uncommon results and service in a most common business." Theirs is a long-term approach with a focus on people first over profits. Peter Clune has helped to continue the legacy, one interaction at a time, valuing every player on the Lockton team.

⑫ THE PIVOT

TOP OF THE 12TH

If 2020 was the year of the pivot due to Covid-19, a different type of shift occurred 100 years earlier, and it had nothing to do with the Spanish flu of 1918.

Andrew "Rube" Foster and seven other African American baseball owners convened at the YMCA in Kansas City, Missouri, with a vision. If black players, equal or better than their white counterparts in talent, were forbidden from taking the same field, Foster and company would just create their own opportunity. They formed the Negro National League on February 13, 1920. "That was the ultimate pivot," said Bob Kendrick, president of the Negro Leagues Baseball Museum.

Let me back up. One of my biggest disappointments professionally is never having met Buck O'Neil, the legendary former player and manager in the Negro Leagues, Major League baseball's first black coach and one of the sport's greatest ambassadors. He passed away at the age of 94 in 2006, less than two years before my arrival in Kansas City. Thankfully, Kendrick is the best storyteller I know and has appeared more frequently on our *Royals Live* television pregame show than any other guest during all of my years broadcasting in KC.

August 16, 2020, started early for Kendrick as he hit the airwaves for a 5 a.m. interview that ran live during a South Korean baseball game. This was the first of many appearances, including two on our broadcast that day, one that would finish for Bob at 10 p.m. after dozens of interviews. Exhausted but filled with gratification, Kendrick had partaken in a national day of recognition to honor the 100th anniversary of the creation of the Negro National League. Every MLB team wore patches, and tributes occurred at stadiums across the country. Sure, there were no fans in the stands due to the pandemic, but the Negro Leagues trended on social media nationally and stole the spotlight all day and night. As Kendrick finished his 17-hour day, he felt the presence of his late friend and mentor Buck O'Neil. "I talk to Buck every day," Kendrick admitted with pride.

Kendrick first met O'Neil in 1993. The former, a volunteer at the Negro Leagues Baseball Museum and the latter, the man who created the institution in Kansas City in 1990. Kendrick recalls initially asking Buck about the motivation in building the museum. The answer was succinct and profound: "So that we would be remembered."

Kendrick said that the August 16 day of celebration resulted in the Negro Leaguers "being remembered in ways I don't even think Buck would have dreamt. It filled you with great pride."

The Negro Leagues comprise one of the most powerful American success stories, all the more inspirational because they thrived during such a shameful period of history. The league became the third-largest black-owned business in the country during the era of segregation. Number one was black-owned insurance companies that provided legitimate coverage for black Americans over inferior policies offered by white carriers. Second was Madam C.J. Walker, who dominated the world of cosmetology in urban areas across the U.S. as she became the country's first self-made female millionaire of any color. The Negro Leagues were third, and influenced black business development in every market they played.

In Kansas City, the Monarchs regularly drew a standing-room-only crowd of more than 17,000. Opening day featured a marching band parading blocks from the 18th and Vine entertainment district (that now houses the museum) to the stadium with all 17,000 following along, marching to the beat of their drum. Forty-thousand fans regularly visited Yankee Stadium to watch the Black Yankees—50,000 for the All-Star Game. Following the contests, the large crowds frequented black-owned restaurants, shops and hotels that all bristled with post-game activity.

Then, there was the action on the field. "Certainly, the most entertaining brand of baseball—and many would argue the best baseball—that was being played, and even more so, they were out-drawing many of those Major League teams," Kendrick said.

For every famous white superstar, a black player of similar or superior talent existed. I've heard Kendrick say numerous times that Josh Gibson was called the black Babe Ruth, but others referred to Ruth as the white Josh Gibson. Buck Leonard compared to Lou Gehrig; Jackie Robinson broke the MLB color barrier; Hank Aaron eclipsed Ruth's all-time home record playing for the Atlanta Braves in 1974; Willie Mays is considered one of the greatest of all time in the majors. All first suited up in the Negro Leagues. To put it in perspective, Kendrick references the late Hall of Famer Monte Irvin, an outfielder who joined MLB's New York Giants in 1949 and mentored a 20-year-old Mays when Mays debuted with the team in 1951: "When I hear someone of [Irvin's] magnitude say 'I played with Willie Mays and I played against Henry Aaron, and neither of them were Josh Gibson,' it makes you wonder, 'How good was Josh Gibson?!'" Translation, Gibson surpassed both legends in talent according to Irvin.

So the ability to overcome adversity and fight through prejudice and forced disadvantage with grace and determination is part of the fabric of the Negro Leagues. It's a spirit the museum channeled in what should have been a special year. It's the spirit of Buck O'Neil.

O'Neil fought year after year for the Negro League greats to be inducted in Major League Baseball's prestigious Hall of Fame. He successfully lobbied and helped open up doors for legendary players who deserved equal standing instead of being excluded. O'Neil himself was expected to earn a spot among baseball's immortals with a vote from a special committee on February 27, 2006. No one knew he would pass away 221 days later, but everyone expected Buck was a lock. Except he inexplicably fell one vote short, and those closest to a man so beloved felt immeasurable pain in their souls. Guess who comforted them? Buck O'Neil. "To see him basically wrap his arms around a room full of people who were mourning, who were angry, who were upset, and there was Buck wrapping his arms around all of us and saying, 'It's okay,'" said Kendrick.

O'Neil told the group, "Y'all just keep on loving Old Buck. If I'm a Hall of Famer in your eyes, that's all that matters to me."

To this day, Kendrick tells me and many others, "I'm still trying to be more Buck-like. I'm a work in progress." He's been tested many times.

While Buck missed the Hall of Fame by one vote, Kendrick, who was the marketing director of the museum, fell short by one vote when the board chose a different president in 2010. He left devastated, forced to depart a place that had become his life. Thirteen months later, with the museum in dire straits and hemorrhaging money, the decision makers asked for a re-do. They wanted Kendrick to return as president. Still hurt by the snub, Kendrick called the decision gut-wrenching. His mind said to move on for good. His heart had other ideas. "The more I tried to be rational and talk myself out of it, Buck was standing over the other shoulder saying, 'Son, come on back home,'" Kendrick said.

When he returned in April of 2011, he estimated the museum had another eight to nine months of operating income. Kendrick raced to plan a critical event in just seven months: Buck O'Neil's 100th Birthday Bash in November. He created an All-Centennial Negro Leagues team and raised $200,000. Momentum continued in 2012 as the Kansas City Royals hosted the MLB All-Star Game. Numerous dignitaries, including Hall of Famers Lou Brock and Dave Winfield, as well as Jackie Robinson's daughter, Sharon Robinson, visited the museum. A year later movie actors Chadwick Boseman and Harrison Ford visited Kansas City for a red-carpet event to promote the movie *42* about Jackie Robinson. That event raised $100,000 for the museum. 2014 and 2015 featured a pair of Royals World Series appearances and subsequently more museum exposure on the national television stage.

Then, more setbacks. It's in the DNA of the Negro Leagues to get knocked down and stand back up. In June 2018, vandals flooded the new Buck O'Neil Education and Research Center, housed in that old YMCA building where it all began for Rube Foster and the Negro Leagues owners. A devastated Kendrick felt ready to give up in that moment. I remember seeing anguish on the face of this usually upbeat man. Hundreds of thousands of dollars worth of damage seemed to be an insurmountable mountain to climb. But Buck had another saying: "People will do bad things. Good people will fix them." The donations and grant money quickly poured in and the project bounced back.

So yes, 2020 was awful. The museum shuttered its doors due to the pandemic for months. Baseball legends and dear friends of the museum Lou Brock, Bob Gibson, Joe Morgan and Chadwick Bozeman, the actor, died within a six-week period. Numerous former Negro League players also passed.

"How do you find a way when there's seemingly no way? That is what I'm most proud of about this museum during the course of this tumultuous year that not only had us dealing with the pandemic, but also social and civil unrest," Kendrick told me in October 2020, as the museum now welcomed a steady stream of masked guests.

The pivot included innovative ideas to keep the museum relevant while its doors remained shut.

A "Tip Your Cap to the Negro Leagues" social media campaign featured four living presidents, NBA greats like Michael Jordan and Magic Johnson, legends from Billie Jean King to famous musicians, actors and everyone in between. It led to a large spike in fundraising.

Congress passed the Negro Leagues Baseball Centennial Commemorative Coin Act, directing the U.S. Treasury to mint a coin that could raise $6 million in future years for the museum.

I tell people visiting Kansas City to make a stop at the Negro Leagues Baseball Museum mandatory on their itinerary. It's a lesson in baseball, history and inspirational pivots of resilience. And if they're lucky, they will catch Bob Kendrick telling stories, carrying on the legacy of a true hero.

Buck O'Neil was the grandson of slaves, and he lived long enough to create change and inspire people along the way. Or as Kendrick said best, "Buck symbolizes everything that is great about this country."

BOTTOM OF THE 12TH

I experienced my own pivot in 2020, just like so many people around the globe in March when the Covid-19 coronavirus altered the world as we knew it. Stressed out and freaked out, I quickly realized that my baseball paychecks would not begin in April. As a freelance broadcaster paid by the game, I was suddenly staring unemployment straight in the eyes.

Jumping on stage to speak to a company would not be an option either with the virus, so that left my weekly podcast, which was not a revenue generator at the time. I needed to pivot, and I found inspiration through different pieces of advice I received from leaders in my business network that I'd met in recent years. (See, that networking pays off in ways that may be greater than money!) Brad Douglas, CEO of Heartland Credit Association, told me to just survive until July. Coincidence or not, we returned to baseball in late July. Denise Mills, a speaker, strategist and facilitator whose words of wisdom always seem to have the Midas touch, suggested I reach out to any companies I had spoken to in the past and offer a free speech. Just a virtual pick-me-up at a time when leaders and their employees needed some inspiration. Mike Matheny, the new Royals manager waiting to direct his team, looked for the positive angle and told me on the phone, "The foundation of care leads to trust and opportunity." That quote resonated every time I shared it with an audience.

My mindset shifted from "How do I make money?" to "Survive and help others." The free speeches gave me practice shifting from stage to virtual and within weeks, companies I did pro bono work for started hiring me to speak to their teams. My podcast also took a new direction. I had wanted to add a video element to the episodes and decided to give it a try. On March 24, I started a Monday-through-Friday live video streaming podcast in addition to the audio version of *Rounding the Bases*. The goal was to help entrepreneurs tell their stories and offer viewers advice and strategies on leadership during a pandemic. Jeff Carson of Enterprise Bank and Trust reached out and wanted to sponsor the show. A partnership formed in promoting the community, and I felt a joint responsibility with Enterprise to make an impact. It felt good to help people stay connected.

On a personal level, listening to my guests made me better. Kathy Nelson, CEO of the Kansas City Sports Commission (featured in Chapter Nine for doing the right thing) shared a powerful phrase from activist Billie Jean King. "Pressure is a privilege." These four words hit me immediately as Kathy expanded on her mindset. "Being asked to help with the city, being asked to help on a national level, being asked to help locally...that's a lot of pressure. It's still such a privilege, and the pressure of being in that room with the Big 12 Men's Basketball Championship and saying we are not going to play men's or women's, that pressure felt very heavy, but I look back and think what a privilege to have a voice."

I understood the privilege of having a voice on my podcast. Guests like Angel McGee of the Royals, André Davis, (Chapter Five) and Drew Eanes, a senior account executive with McKinstry, gave me a deeper understanding of racial injustice issues plaguing our country following George Floyd's death in Minneapolis. I found a purpose and platform to allow others to share their perspectives. A time of pressure led to a renewed focus on empathy and listening in a season when so many people seemed to be arguing.

We returned to baseball on July 24, broadcasting road games from an empty Kauffman Stadium. Not an easy task connecting with players and creating content via Zoom, but it sure beat sitting at home. My daily saying was "the show goes on," and viewers at home didn't care about the challenges of broadcasting baseball with reduced player access, so pivoting and embracing the protocol was critical. Leveraging years' worth of trust built with players enabled me to remain productive in my role as a reporter. Royals Vice President of Media Relations Mike Swanson and his staff worked above and beyond to keep us connected—a true team effort.

The best pivot story featured on my podcast came from a businessman who thought he might go under. Husband and father of one with another child on the way, Andy Rieger looked like a man lacking sleep as he joined me on the video podcast April 3. Four months earlier, he and I had sat together for dinner at a holiday party in the Hey! Hey! Supper Club in the basement of J. Rieger and Company's brand-new, 65,000 square foot, three-story building that included multiple bars, rentable space for private events and a distillery that produced whiskey, gin, amaro and vodka. But by March, Andy's thriving business had hit the Covid wall. No more parties, no more guests, and bar and liquor store clients across the country lacked a need for Rieger products due to nationwide closures.

"It's easily the craziest time period that we could've ever imagined in life," Andy told me just days after closing his facility to the public. J. Rieger and Co. employed 95 people. Andy promised to pay everyone for two weeks initially as the shutdown began. Some chose to leave and collect unemployment. About 65 wanted to stay full time.

Andy's Rieger ancestors knew all about adversity. Jacob Rieger, Andy's great-great-great-grandfather had immigrated to the United States from Austria-Hungary in 1877. After initially settling in Cincinnati, Jacob and his family moved to Kansas City in the early 1880s, where he opened a grocery store. In 1887, Jacob started making alcohol and founded J. Rieger & Co. in a neighborhood located on the Missouri/Kansas border. Prohibition already existed in Kansas, so J. Rieger & Co. drew many customers from both sides of the state line to a neighborhood in Missouri that was suddenly booming with restaurants, hotels and casinos. Jacob's son Alexander took over the business in 1900 and began offering mail-order services for its products, shipping alcohol all over the country to more than 250,000 customers. J. Rieger & Co. became a huge national brand, hailing itself as the largest wholesale whiskey distributor in the United States. They sent out fliers that appeared in newspapers, asking for customers to send $3 in an envelope to the distillery in Kansas City in exchange for a gallon of whiskey, plus a free pint and gift shot glass. Three weeks later, the package would arrive to the customer. In 1915, Alexander opened the Rieger hotel near the train station, offering affordable rates to blue-collar business travelers and railway workers. A mural on the building featuring a bottle of Rieger's whiskey advertised to every guest passing through. Business boomed until the 18th Amendment was passed in 1919, making the production, sale, and transport of intoxicating liquors illegal nationwide. Alexander shut down J. Rieger & Co. by the end of 1919. He and his son Nathan, Andy's grandfather, opened a bank and excelled with their pivot.

In December 2009, Andy, a Kansas City native, found a job in Dallas as an investment banker a month after graduating early from SMU. Andy's dad, Tom, was diagnosed with Stage IV cancer soon after in May and passed away in August 2010. Tom had ironically found his first job at a bank in Dallas after graduating from college in California many years before. Six months after he'd started work, Tom's mom had been diagnosed with cancer and soon died. He returned home to Kansas City to spend time with his father, regretting not having moved back earlier for the final days of his mom's life. When Tom Rieger got sick in 2010, he told Andy, "Whatever happens to me, do not move home because of my fate. Only move back to Kansas City if there's ever a real reason to move back," Andy recalled.

Prior to his death, Tom sent Andy an article from the Kansas City Star about how the old Rieger Hotel (long out of the hands of the Rieger family) was going to reopen as a restaurant called The Rieger on the first floor of the old hotel building. "My dad said to me, 'If I'm not around when this opens, make sure you go as the only Rieger around and help them if they need help.'" Andy returned home to visit his mom over Christmas that year and stopped by the restaurant multiple times to bring family pictures for display on the wall to honor the Rieger history. Owner Ryan Maybee had been digging deeper into the background of the building and discovered the J. Rieger & Co story. "All of a sudden my mind was blown, and I was like, wow, there was a distillery in Kansas City that made whiskey in the 1800s," Maybee told me as my sixth-ever audio podcast guest. Ryan had no connection to the family prior to meeting Andy. His Rieger knowledge came from a heavy dose of curiosity, 21st century style. "This was all a result of Google," Maybee said laughing.

He recalls opening week for the restaurant and visits from a stranger named Andy Rieger. "He just said 'Hey, I wanted to congratulate you and wish you well.' He didn't really want anything at all aside from just saying good luck and this is really cool." During Andy's third visit, Maybee threw it out there, telling the Rieger family's only living descendant at the time, "We should partner together and resurrect your family's distillery." Ryan remembers the reaction, or at least the body language from Andy as saying, "I don't know you. You're crazy."

Maybee kept mulling over what he considered a romantic idea to bring back a Prohibition-era distillery. He knew that including a family member would make the story more authentic, so he kept developing the idea. Andy went to lunch with Ryan during another trip home to KC in 2011 and they discussed re-opening J. Rieger & Co. Andy looked over business plans primarily as a third party offering friendly advice. Happy with a successful finance career, Andy had no interest in being involved in the old family business, but found himself more connected as details evolved. Back in Dallas in the summer of 2013, he discussed J. Rieger & Co. with his future wife, Lucy. "She goes, 'I think this is what your dad was talking about. I think he was literally referencing this scenario. That this is what you're supposed to do.' Lucy was like, 'I think we're supposed to move to Kansas City,'" Rieger said. He knew this could be the opportunity of a lifetime and in April of 2014, Andy left the world of finance and moved back home to KC with Lucy. J. Rieger and Co. launched half a year later, producing whiskey to start. The distillery was housed in a small warehouse attached to an unused old brewery. Lack of space became an issue, so they bought the adjacent old Heim Brewery, which was originally built in 1901 and was also a casualty of Prohibition. The spectacular new facility opened in July of 2019. J. Rieger & Co. quickly became a destination and trendy choice for holiday parties and corporate events over the winter...until Covid-19 arrived. Another Rieger pivot followed.

How would J. Rieger & Co. keep its 60+ employees working? They brainstormed to-go cocktails, food packages and revamped retail, all of which helped, but one specific product tipped the scales. Hand sanitizer! They already had the materials, so Rieger employees started working around the clock to produce hand sanitizer for the community, businesses, hospitals and nursing home facilities.

Wearing a Rieger hoodie with the "O! So Good" marketing slogan from the early 1900s on it during our podcast, Andy told me about the range of emotions he and his staff experienced, going from survival to possible failure to being inspired by personal stories from customers. They learned of elderly relatives unable to leave the house, out of soap and in desperate need of hand sanitizer that Rieger's company now provided. These stories from strangers often came through tears.

The initial goal was just to keep the lights on. As cars started to arrive in long lines to pick up the hand sanitizer, the pivot became powerful, renewing faith in the human spirit at such a dark and challenging time. Andy had just finished handing out a bottle on an early March morning to a customer, the emotions of that person's plight affecting him as he moved through the line. "I go up to the next car, wipe my tears away and the guy goes, 'Hey, here's $100. I just need one bottle. Will you please use the rest of this money to take care of your employees and take care of other people that have needs?'" Another man pulled up asking for 600 bottles for his business. "He goes, 'But I would like to pay for 700,'" Andy recalled. The community responded to the J. Rieger pivot in a way that made employees at the distillery feel like they had a purpose greater than their role.

I asked Andy months later if J. Rieger & Co. could have survived without the hand sanitizer. The answer was a quick and emphatic "no," not without letting employees go. As the pandemic rolled on during the year, the distillery worked on new products. They also saw a rise in their distribution of whiskey and other spirits, even at a time of closures. Andy Rieger does not see himself as an entrepreneur—doesn't even like the word—but prefers to be viewed as a contrarian. He likes to go against the grain. While everyone else is doing one thing, he's doing something else. "Playing chess while others play checkers," as he put it. To recap the Mike Matheny quote, "The foundation of care leads to trust and opportunity." J. Rieger and Co. passed that test and it was O! So Good.

 **PASS IT ON**

TOP OF THE 13TH

---

*"It's important to leave the world in better shape
than when you came into it."*

—WILLIAM H. DUNN SR.

John Ernest Dunn Sr., a.k.a. Ernie, played semi-professional baseball as a pitcher in the Pacific Coast League in his early twenties while working as a lighting supply salesman in the off-season. He started JE Dunn construction doing housing and general construction jobs in 1924 based on hard work, philanthropy and integrity. His son, Bill Dunn, Sr., excelled as a pitcher, too. Fun fact about Bill: He competed against future baseball big leaguers Yogi Berra and Joe Garagiola as a kid in Legion Ball.

Nearly 100 years later, JE Dunn operates at a much larger level, but continues to follow the guiding principles that began with its founders—focusing on families first, doing the right thing and serving others. During WWII, JE Dunn took on government contracts and made significant money, but out of respect for the war effort, Dunn chose to give the savings on the job back to the federal government, earning him praise from President Franklin D. Roosevelt.

Bill Dunn Sr. began working for his dad before the war and eventually bought the company years later, after his father's death. I had the opportunity to eat lunch at the JE Dunn offices in 2018 with the second, third and fourth generations of Dunns, and talked about the company culture. Mr. Dunn, Chairman Emeritus and in his 90s at that point, still came to work three days per week and led a spirited discussion about baseball that day.

Bill's son, Terry, joined JE Dunn in 1974 and went on to lead the company for 25 years, putting it firmly on the map by growing its presence around the country by nearly 400 percent in the 1990s. He told me "as you build an entity, the most important strategy you have is the values and culture."

I first met Terry Dunn in January of 2018. Soft spoken but intense, authoritative but caring, the highly accomplished executive took an immediate interest in my career. Within moments of walking into his office, he was offering me guidance regarding my new speaking endeavors. He began drawing a detailed business plan on a white board and was designing ideas like an offensive coordinator in football. The words "vision," "mission," "strategies," "structure," "capital," and "measurement" filled the board. I was overwhelmed initially, but transfixed by his attention to detail, passion and interest in sharing his knowledge with me.

I have to admit that the day we met, I felt a small bit of skepticism only in the sense that it's rare in the television world for someone to offer help and advice without an agenda. What could such a powerhouse figure like Terry Dunn receive from helping me? I came to learn quickly that Terry understands the need to pass on life's knowledge to those he believes could benefit. Many conversations later, he told me, "It's one of the most important things I have to offer. I don't have the answers, but I think I can raise the right questions with people when we sit down and visit."

Like his father and grandfather, Terry excelled on the athletic fields, playing baseball in college at Rockhurst College in Kansas City, although football was his favorite. He had many mentors along the way, from his dad, to coaches, to people he met in the construction world, where he truly learned to compete while working on job sites as a teenager. A physically strong all-state football player, young Terry once decided to pick up and carry two shores, which weighed 50 to 60 pounds each. The task called for him to take one, but doubling the load presented no issues for a tough kid. He wanted to prove he belonged and was not just the boss's son receiving a handout. The foreman sat him down afterward and said, "I know you can do it. You can carry two shores, but you got about four or five other guys on your crew, and they're going to get very ticked off if they see you are way outworking them." He recalled that story, knowing the mentorship he received that day helped him understand roles, the importance of being a team player and earning the respect of teammates.

Terry never thought he would lead the construction company. After college, he actually worked two years in the banking industry as he pursued a master's degree in business. He joined JE Dunn as a contract officer in 1974 and was named chief executive officer in 1989, a role he served until 2013.

By the time I met Terry, he had retired from JE Dunn, but there's really no such thing as retirement for this man. He's regularly investing in businesses and people and always trying to solve some of society's most significant issues. From workforce development for people coming out of prison to tackling issues of affordable housing and helping to build equity and spark home ownership in urban communities to providing mentorship programs for young African

American males...he's busy. Not to mention all of the philanthropic endeavors he and his wife, Peggy, the mayor of Leawood, Kansas, lead.

His desire to mentor did not start later in life for Terry. Katie Dunn Fitzgerald, Principal and Senior Wealth Consultant at Mariner Wealth Advisors, is one of the best connectors in Kansas City, in my opinion. I should know. Katie has introduced me to so many influential people over the years... including her father, Terry. She received a lifetime's worth of wisdom from the man I've begun to learn from in recent years. "My dad has always been one of my mentors. He taught me to never give up on your dreams and passions. If you put in the hard work, discipline and effort, you will be rewarded," she said. "Always put faith and family first and remember the whole reason we are on this earth is to ultimately get to heaven. So, make all decisions in life and business with this in mind."

I now have pages and pages of notes from every meeting with Terry, and they match Katie's comments. He sees five key values or virtues that are all equally important in anything anyone does in life. "Faith," which is your belief in your core values. "Hope" is a vision to change tomorrow. "Love" is a passion or commitment, also known as "paying the price." And finally, "Integrity" and "Trust," which can be often overlooked, but both tie everything else together. Dunn said there can be other elements, but these five must be included. "If you understand this chemistry of integrity and trust, it's a 24/7… you've got to just be totally engaged and encourage that level [of engagement] with your team. If you do, the magic is that each one of them can become a leader in his or her own way."

My biggest memory from that initial January 10, 2018, meeting was Terry's perfect grasp of who I was as a person within moments of my walking into the room. Sure, he was an avid baseball fan who watched my broadcasts, but how could he know me so well? This wasn't some psychic grasping at a vague concept that seemed to conveniently fit my profile. How did he know about my humility and my ability to break down barriers with others? (His words, not mine.) Dunn explained to me about the need for a CEO to observe from 30,000 feet (translation: read people) while being down on the floor with the day-to-day activity. "Ninety-nine percent of a CEO's job is to listen," he told me. (A common theme from executives throughout this book.) He hadn't just watched me on television. He had observed me from a distance and correctly assessed me. I was sold on this man immediately, and while I never asked him to officially be my mentor, he became a calming force and source of knowledge for me. He talked to me about trust and advised me not to change my brand, reminding me that it's who I am. He also emphasized the importance of storytelling. "Anybody that has a challenge, I really want them to own and tell their own story. If I can help them write that story, that's great. They've got to own it. If they want to bounce ideas off me, I will give that to them." Dunn further explained, "The story typically starts with a vision. What do you want to do? Where are you going? A mission is what you do every day to try to achieve that. Then, you get into the strategies, the structure, the capital, whatever you need—business plan or whatever, and then you have to have a measurement. You have to be able to ask the question, 'Am I doing what I said I was going to do, and if not, why not?'"

Dunn's secret is to listen while also thinking multiple steps ahead. This is a skill that can be developed, and he believes the best leaders can do it six steps ahead on any decision. "It's almost like a fighter pilot. Going into combat and not only thinking about your next reaction, but what are your multiple reactions," Dunn told me on the podcast. As a newer speaker often too hyper-focused on landing that next gig early on, Terry taught me to think big picture and to aim higher. Provide value and play a role in helping companies develop a winning strategy as a change agent through trust. This all seemed so lofty for a guy just hoping to motivate people through some speeches, until it started to make sense and happen. I began thinking six steps ahead.

These days, the Dunn family values ring truer than ever. Gordon Lansford now serves as JE Dunn's first non-Dunn family CEO while Tim Dunn, JE's great-grandson and Terry's nephew, is the chairman of the board. The JE Dunn Employee Stock Ownership Plan was created in 2010 with employees joining after one year of working full time and becoming fully vested after six years.

Tim said of the ownership plan: "It accelerated some very positive cultural impacts to the company that enhanced the values to guiding principles. This was transformational because we also became an employee-focused company as much as a client-focused company. It's made a major impact in 10 years to innovation, collaboration, attracting key talent, etc."

In November of 2019 Dunn employees learned they would hold more than a piece of the company. The Kansas City Royals had just been sold. The Dunn Family and JE Dunn Construction would be a part of the ownership group.

Lansford and Tim Dunn broke the news to their staff with a message: "As an employee-owner of JE Dunn, you now share in the ownership of the Kansas City Royals," the note said. "The baseball bug has stayed in the Dunns' hearts over several generations. The Royals are a KC community treasure and we are proud, humbled, and inspired to be involved. For our employees outside of KC, we know you'll continue to love your team, but we hope the Royals can be in your hearts as well!"

Sitting for another lunch with Terry Dunn about a year later, we talked about baseball. Less about the results of the recently completed season and more about the team's needs. He spoke with no hint of having an ownership stake in the team and more as a knowledgeable observer with a view from 30,000 feet, talking about offseason needs for not just the next season but many years to come. Always six steps ahead, while sharing his knowledge with a student hungry to learn.

BOTTOM OF THE 13TH

As Sandy Kemper and I discussed, I believe that an organization with a strong culture usually has one word attached to its name: "Way." Allow me to explain. When I left St. Louis in 2008 after nearly 10 years of working in that market, I didn't fully understand why the Cardinals won so frequently in baseball. Sure, they had talent, but it was more than that. They *expected* to win, and not just on the field. In the community. Their success included everyone involved with the team, and their pride showed. When I arrived in Kansas City for what would be the best and most significant move of my career, I stepped into an organization that had been the polar opposite of the Cardinals in terms of wins and interest. St. Louis had won the fifth-most games of all 30 teams in baseball with a record of 894-734 during my tenure working in eastern Missouri. During that same stretch, the Kansas City Royals won 200 fewer games than their in-state rivals and suffered the second-most losses in baseball.

I remember being a visiting broadcaster at Kauffman Stadium in Kansas City during the 2007 season while traveling with the Cardinals. I knew then that this beautiful stadium could be my future home. I had expressed interest to my boss back in St. Louis about moving to KC in 2008 as Fox Sports was going to be taking over the rights to broadcast Royals games. A personal connection to Kansas City made the move even more appealing; my wife had grown up there before her family moved away when she was 11 years old. By 2007, trips to Kansas City were already part of our life. My sister-in-law, brother-in-law, niece and nephew lived there, so we spent many holidays and birthdays driving across Missouri. Someone in the family asked if my interest in the potential job was just so we could be closer to them: "You know the Royals aren't very good, right?" I assured them that this was a better job than my current role. The allure was more airtime and responsibility for me, and the chance to go from back-up host and reporter to host and reporter on every broadcast.

So, while visiting KC with the Cardinals in June of 2007, I introduced myself to Dayton Moore on the field at Kauffman Stadium. The Royals general manager, who had taken over the reins of this struggling franchise about a year before, had been tasked with making a once-proud organization relevant again. I vividly recall asking Dayton his hopes and goals and he told me he wanted to build a championship culture. He said he didn't just mean the 25 players in the locker room. He meant the ticket takers, the ushers, the vendors, the fans—and not just the fans in Kansas City, but around the region and beyond. I thought to myself, "Sounds great, but...good luck!" I knew the numbers, all those losses. I didn't know about the desire and determination of a man who could change a city. Back then, there was no "Royals Way." Not yet, anyway. But the greatest part of my move to KC, outside of Susan and me raising our kids in an amazing community we now cherish as our home, has been watching this organization find its way. A genuine culture followed, as did success on the field. I received a front-row seat and master class education in building culture from an expert—Dayton Moore.

Dayton had learned from one of his mentors, John Schuerholz. Schuerholz led the Royals to success in the 1980s and then built the Atlanta Braves as general manager in the 1990s and early 2000s.

"If you want mentors in your life, you have to be open and accepting and allow people to speak truth, mold you, shape you," said Moore.

I've watched Dayton over the years go from a hungry, passionate leader to something more. A man who's found an even greater purpose. Players look at him as a father as much as they do a boss. One of the many elements of culture I've learned from him is the importance of listening to people and understanding them at a deeper level.

I've also learned about the power of passing it on from players...and unlikely ones at that.

I've interviewed hundreds and hundreds of personalities over the years. Some of them fall into the "nicest guy in the world" category, others fit labels like "most fun," "smartest", "best talker," "worst talker," and everything in between.

There was something different about Yordano Ventura to me, though. I can't remember the moment that it clicked, but he just had this huge smile (the smile always gets me) and infectious personality that transcended any language barrier. I recognized early on that "Ace" Ventura spoke much better English than he realized. Like so many of the Latin American Royals players, Ventura learned English from a teacher in Arizona named Monica Ramirez (profiled in Chapter Nine). Yordano ruffled feathers on the field. Throwing 100 miles per hour up near the head did not please the opposition, and this young, wild stallion sparked numerous brawls on the mound. His teammates would privately express their frustration to me, but then quickly talk about loving him. He was the classic little brother. Ace could walk into the clubhouse with the odd ensemble of expensive Gucci dress shoes, a polo shirt and basketball shorts and have the room in stitches with his appearance. Add to that a distinct voice that could pierce a loud room in an energetic way, and he left everyone feeling good.

I wanted so badly to profile his personality, but he insisted on speaking in Spanish for an interview while using a translator. I've thought about this challenge often in my career. What if I went to work in another country, studied the local language and then found myself in a situation surrounded by cameras and microphones, tasked with speaking to reporters? There's no way! But I knew Ace's personality would endear him to fans and that his English more than passed the test for an interview minus a translator. So, with some nudging from Monica (I don't think he ever knew that I was asking her to lobby on my behalf), he agreed to do his first-ever English interview without help. Just the two of us in a room with my photographer. I locked the door because I knew his teammates would likely try to interrupt by making faces or distracting him. Boys will be boys with their pranks. I can't count how many times Ace would stand behind our camera during a game as I reported live from the dugout, making faces or throwing sunflower seeds at me to try and mess me up, all the while flashing a gargantuan and slightly devilish smile. This was the personality I wanted to share. I promised him that day, "I won't let you fail." I even typed up a list of questions in the notes section of my phone that I still have to this day. Simple questions like: "What's it like playing in the big leagues?" "How old were you when you started dreaming of baseball?" "Who were your favorite players as a kid?"

So, we rehearsed. I'm generally someone who prefers spontaneity but didn't want him to have to deal with any surprises because he was practically shaking from nervousness. My goal was to make him comfortable and allow his personality to shine. Ventura began to gain confidence during the course of the interview and settled in beautifully. What transpired following that day was a willingness to do interviews with me, or with me and my partner, Jeff Montgomery,

without a translator. His growing trust in me allowed me to share with fans a playful, loving Yordano Ventura. (For a glimpse of his personality, just Google "Yordano Ventura ooh baby," a clip that went viral.)

Ace did numerous interviews with us on Fox Sports prior to passing away in a tragic car accident in his native Dominican Republic in January of 2017. I remember reading the news while lying in bed early on a Sunday morning, just hoping the reports on Twitter were erroneous. As officials and the Royals confirmed the worst nightmare, a team and community began to mourn the loss of a 25-year-old who had told friends that 2017 would be his breakout year as a pitcher.

I took solace and pride in all those interviews we'd shared, but my biggest takeaway about Ventura came from a story in 2016 that I never fully understood until after his death. During spring training of that year, our special projects producer Colleen Lotz asked me to interview a number of pitchers for a story previewing the rotation. She's always been a master at putting these shows together, but she doesn't live in Kansas City or spend much time around the team, so she asked me who I would recommend for interviews. I suggested a number of guys, including Ventura. As the person responsible for putting the pieces of this show together, Colleen reasonably asked me if Yordano's English was easy to understand. I proudly told her "yes," but then ran into an issue: He brought teammate Jorge Bonifacio with him to the interview and refused to answer my questions unless he was sitting on Bonifacio's lap. Not wanting to be insulting or rude, Colleen quietly asked me who the other player was, and when I explained that "Boni" was a minor-league outfielder, I could see from her reaction that even the greatest of producers couldn't fit the pieces of the puzzle together on this one. How can we preview the pitching staff with a starter sitting on the lap of an outfielder who had never played in the big leagues? But Ace stubbornly refused to budge, so I handed him the microphone and said, "Just interview each other." And they did.

I figured it was just classic Ventura, messing with me once again. It ran its course and Bonifacio went on his way, allowing me to complete the originally planned portion of the Q&A. I never thought more about it until I started hearing stories at a memorial for Ventura 11 months later. I learned that he used to visit the room of younger, Spanish-speaking teammates on the road to help them order room service late at night after a game. They were too afraid they would be misunderstood on the phone and Ace loved to play the role of mentor. It dawned on me that he wasn't playing with me that day with Bonifacio in Arizona. Having reached a comfort level of being interviewed in English, he wanted to share his expertise with a young, up-and-coming fellow Dominican and give Boni the experience of sitting in front of a television camera. When Bonifacio made his MLB debut in Arlington, Texas, four months following his mentor's death, he did so with confidence and a smile, no doubt thinking about his late friend Yordano Ventura. Yordano had passed on his expertise. Bonifacio learned something invaluable from Ventura in that moment. So did I. We should never stop observing and absorbing.

Even leaders like Dayton Moore are constantly looking for opportunities to grow. He always tries to hold himself accountable and listen to others. Sitting in his office on the sixth floor at Kauffman Stadium, the now-longtime Royals general manager told me there's inspiration to pull from in every direction. "Everybody up and down this hallway I get motivation from at different times of the year, different times of the day, different times in my career. I've been inspired by many people." He went on to explain that these impactful moments can come from anyone, like the upbeat parking lot attendant who greets employees and fans with a positive message. "That lifts me up. What does that do in return? In return, it motivates me to give back. It motivates me to be kind. It motivates me to have simple kindness and concern for others."

Moore explained further that everyone is capable of passing on what they know to improve a team, community and culture. "You get to a point in your life where you realize that it's all about the next generation, but you have to ask yourself what do you want society, your community, your family, your country to look like for your kids and grandkids. Whatever you want it to look like, you need to model it because leadership is caught, it's not taught."

In January of 2014, Moore founded the C You in the Major Leagues Foundation to support youth baseball, education, faith-based organizations and events, and families in crisis throughout the greater Kansas City area and beyond.

Another vision of Moore's came to fruition in March of 2018 with the opening of the Kansas City MLB Urban Youth Academy, a non-profit organization with the mission to empower kids through baseball, softball, academic and social opportunities to be the leaders of the future.

The employees and the many kids passing through the hallways and taking the field inside and outside at this pristine facility are treated like any member of the Kansas City Royals. Dayton Moore did once tell me he wanted everyone to be a part of the culture.

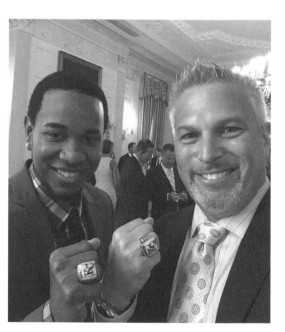

It's the Royals Way.

POSTGAME

I was walking out to left field to our *Royals Live* set before a night game...late, once again. Our crew likes us to sit down well before the start of the show to make final preparations and review elements. In his book, *If These Walls Could Talk*, my longtime broadcast partner Jeff Montgomery wrote about our on-air chemistry, but also noted one large difference between us: "We're like the Odd Couple, though. I have the old baseball mentality that if you're five minutes early, you're late. So, for a 6:30 airtime, I'm on the set by 6:10. Joel oftentimes is really late. Sometimes it's out of his control—usually not."

He's right; but on this day, I had a legit excuse. On my way, I had bumped into owner David Glass who was surrounded by half a dozen guests. He introduced me to the man standing closest to him as Doug McMillon, the CEO of Walmart. I then turned to say "hello" to the next man without seeing his face. As I heard his voice and looked him in the eye, I suddenly realized one of my longtime news heroes was staring back at me. "I'm Tom Brokaw. Nice to meet you, Joel." *Didn't expect that, but I've got to get going out to left field,* I thought.

Mr. Glass had other ideas. "Joel, tell them the Walmart pants story," I heard. Straight from the mouth of the owner of the Royals...the CEO of Walmart and Tom Brokaw awaited.

Here goes: It was July 20, 2016. We left Kauffman Stadium on buses to the airport following a Royals afternoon loss. Scheduled to fly on the team charter for a rare one-day trip, the Royals organization was traveling to Washington, D.C. and the White House to be honored for our previous season's World Championship. We were allowed to bring our spouses.

On the bus, our broadcast partner Steve Physioc was freaking out. Phiz is a longtime broadcaster known equally for his loving personality and his big calls on television. He's hands down the nicest human being and most selfless teammate any broadcaster could have. None of my colleagues would debate that statement. Poor Phiz had left his beautiful, fancy, expensive World Series ring at the stadium, perhaps in the bathroom, he thought. The bus wasn't turning around and we were D.C. bound. I truly felt awful for him.

When we got to the hotel, I unpacked Susan's dress, my suit coat, shirt and tie. All good except...I FORGOT TO PACK DRESS PANTS! It was after 9 p.m., and we had to be in the lobby by 7 a.m. sharp before leaving for the White House. Now *I* was freaking out, suddenly as nervous as Phiz without his ring. I couldn't attend a formal ceremony at the White House in jeans, which was what I was wearing and all I had. I started envisioning trips to random towns in Virginia or anywhere that might have a store open that sold dress pants at odd hours. Susan began searching online for clothing stores open late and found one in the District. Walmart!!! We took an Uber, arrived eight minutes before the store closed and found a pair of khakis.

The next morning, we walked onto the White House lawn and you know my wife told everyone who would listen that I was wearing inexpensive Walmart pants. As we waited in the security line, Rex Hudler walked up to me. Bouncing up and down with his usual off-the-charts energy, Hud said to me in a hushed voice, "Goldy, take this ring," as he handed me his championship ring.

I said, "Hud, I don't need your ring, I have my own ring," as I flashed my bling.

His reply: "It's not mine. It's Physioc's. I stole it yesterday." Poor Phiz had put his ring down at Kauffman Stadium and Hud swiped it. (Or, as I learned years later, it may have been Mr. Innocent Ryan Lefebvre who did the dirty work.) But Hud gave it to ME.

"Why me?" I asked. Hud referenced a visit I had made to 1600 Pennsylvania Ave. the year before as a guest of Royals fan and White House Press Secretary Josh Earnest. Not letting the truth get in the way of a good Hudism, Hud said, "Didn't you meet the Secretary of State last year?" "*Secretary of State, Press Secretary. Whatever. Classic Hud*," I thought and then corrected him with a laugh. He continued. "Yeah, yeah, Press Secretary. Well, you know him, right? Bring Phiz's ring to him and ask him to have Obama announce that he has Phiz's ring. We can embarrass Phiz in front of the whole world!" So, now I was in on it. I walked through Secret Service, and the bullet-proof glass, and the bomb-sniffing dogs with over $35,000 worth of jewelry bought by Mr. Glass while wearing a $14 pair of pants from Walmart, the company he used to lead. I gave the ring to Earnest, who promptly proceeded to present it to Phiz, taking President Obama off the hook. He said something about the Royals giving him a ring due to his superfan status but the name "Physioc" mysteriously being engraved on it.

Mr. Glass loved that story. Doug McMillon and Tom Brokaw both laughed as I made my way to the set with my crew forgiving me for being late, again. I could replace the ring story with hundreds of others. We have so much fun. Something happens every day with our broadcast crew that represents Small Ball. Trust, positivity, attention to detail, every role matters. We hit curveballs daily because live television never goes as planned. Kind of like life.

———

After a four-month hiatus due to the coronavirus pandemic, we finally returned to work July 24, 2020. Walking in with a required mask, I entered an empty stadium with no baseball activity anywhere to be seen at the complex. The season opener took place in Cleveland, and we would spend the abbreviated schedule working both home and road games from Kauffman Stadium. No access to players in locker rooms or on the field. The ability to overhear conversations

taking place below while sitting in the broadcast booth above just became part of the routine. Was it weird with no fans and piped-in crowd noise? Yes...until it became normal. Routine settled in, and it felt great to be back. Although I found myself stressed out one week, working on too many projects at once. A friend reminded me to enjoy the games and not take any of it for granted. Which made me think of a quote I once saw from longtime baseball player and manager Clint Hurdle, who said, "Be where your feet are. Enjoy the moment. There'll be a day when there won't be another day." When I first saw those words years ago, I began a ritual of always making sure to feel the grass beneath my feet when I walked off the field following a postgame interview. While I never stepped foot on the perfectly manicured lawn of Kauffman Stadium in 2020, my heart and mind fully embraced the privilege of bringing people together through baseball. Just like the daily pandemic podcast conversations. If pressure is indeed a privilege, as Billie Jean King said, I understood my role of celebrating the big results achieved from Small Ball.

ACKNOWLEDGMENTS

I could write another book just acknowledging every person who has impacted my life every step of the way along this journey, but I hope to single out a few here.

When I was 15 years old, I applied for a job at a local restaurant named Michael's in the Chicago suburbs. I spent eight years working there, through high school and summers at home from college cooking, cleaning, prepping food and doing anything asked of me. I learned how to grill the best tasting hot dogs on the planet, but more significantly, I received a lifetime's education on the importance of people, customer relations, teamwork and hard work. This all just reinforced lessons learned from my mom, Nancy, and my dad, Alan. As latchkey kids of the 1980s, my brother Marc and I woke up every weekday with our parents already downtown at their offices. They arrived home well after we returned from school. We knew no other way. The long hours put in at Michael's and always treating people well and with respect reflected the values my parents instilled in us, values I still live by to this day.

I'm lucky enough to brag about four parents. Sign me up in the rare club of people who adore their in-laws. Larry and Judy are my second father and mother and I count my blessings to have two families I love equally.

More on my personal crew in a moment, but from a professional standpoint, I've worked with countless men and women every step along the way who taught me about the significance of every role on a team. This includes the biggest-name athletes and those behind the scenes making it all work. Our move to KC enabled me to truly realize my broadcast dreams. The Glass family and Dayton Moore supported me every step of the way. I also want to thank Mike Swanson. There's no better media relations person in baseball so having Swanee and his staff as a daily resource is a luxury most reporters could only hope to have at their fingertips.

I highlighted numerous influences and mentors in my speaking and podcasting career throughout the book. I want to single out Casey Wright, Scott Havens and Matt Benge for opening door after door for me. Barb Teicher, Steven Iwerson, Mary Redmond, Lauren Schieffer and my many National Speakers Association friends all helped mold me on stage.

I hired Danielle Welch as my marketing manager in the summer of 2018 and she's built my brand and taught me every step of the way. Colleen Lotz joined my team in 2020 to edit my podcasts. Colleen and I began working together at Fox Sports Midwest in 2006, and I trust her and value her opinion as much as any colleague I've worked with in my career.

Jeff Landsman and I started hanging out together as eighth graders in 1986. Afternoons after high school were often spent with us pretending to be DJs as we recorded shows. Jeff would also record me doing mock television newscasts. Eventually I became the TV guy and he went on to work for Oprah as an editor. Today, he owns his own production company and our lifelong friendship also includes regular pep talks for each other as we jointly navigate the world of entrepreneurship. There's no better friend, and I make that statement in spite of having failed at convincing Jeff to love sports for about 35 years and counting.

Paige DeRuyscher and I met the way many people did during a pandemic…on a Zoom call. I cannot think of a more kind, caring and invested editor and project partner than Paige. I felt an instant chemistry with her and am proud to have worked on this book with Paige. Her positive vibes put me at ease every day writing this book.

Thanks to Kerri Holtzman, the wife of Dave Holtzman from our TV crew. Kerri lent her copywriting expertise to my book and I was amazed, but not surprised, at her attention to detail.

The three most important people in my life have put up with my hectic and unique schedule every day of their lives so please allow me to brag about my wife and kids before I wrap up. Mason and Ellie remind me every day that I'm just dad, not a TV personality. Eye rolls and sarcastic autograph requests are part of their routine in keeping me humble. I reciprocate with awful "Dad jokes."

Mason is my mini-me in every way, except he towers over me by a good four inches. I've watched him grow more than just physically these last couple of years. Mason's perseverance makes me proud in a way I can't fully express. I should apologize to him for passing on my athletic genes but his big personality and positive energy make him the perfect teammate.

Ellie does things every day that make me smile. She's one of the funniest people I know. Caring like her brother, and so talented as an actress and singer. I never expected we would have a daughter, but it sure is awesome being a girl dad. I don't know where the straight A's came from. Maybe her mother?

Sitting in the audience watching Ellie on stage or Mason on the ice playing hockey is as good as it gets for me. What true joy for a parent.

My kids would be nothing without Susan. I can say the same thing for me. I knew I would be marrying an amazing woman when I proposed in 1998. She had just said yes to the question I had taped on her graduation cap, "Will you marry me?" Having agreed to join my crazy world permanently, Susan walked on to the football field at Northwestern University, newly engaged, and about to celebrate her completion of graduate school. Justice Ruth Bader Ginsburg delivered an inspiring commencement speech. Susan would be my source of inspiration going forward. Always in my corner, my wife has supported a career that allowed me to live my dream, often at the expense of our family. The Goldbergs become a family of three during baseball season every year as I travel across the country and they always make it work. It's our life for better and worse, and Susan makes it all happen around or in spite of my schedule. This family would be lost without her. I always knew she would be the best mother and wife and I'm proven correct daily. The sports and broadcast world can tear loved ones apart with the odd hours and abnormal routine, but Susan has kept us together. She's more comfortable in the background and with me in the spotlight, so we complement each other well. She's the true superstar.

Thanks to everyone along the way for the support. It's been a privilege to write about Small Ball and the little things that lead to big results.